LIGHTING DESIGN SOURCEBOOK

First published in the United States of America by
Rockport Publishers, Inc.
33 Commercial Street
Gloucester, Massachusetts 01930-5089
Telephone: (978) 282-9590
Fax: (978) 283-2742
www.rockpub.com

Library of Congress Cataloging-in-Publication data available

ISBN 1-56496-929-0
10 9 8 7 6 5 4 3 2 1
Cover Design: Wilson Harvey
Cover Images: Randall Whitehead

Printed in China
Printed in Hong Kong

LIGHTING DESIGN
SOURCEBOOK

**600 SOLUTIONS FOR
RESIDENTIAL AND
COMMERCIAL SPACES**

RANDALL WHITEHEAD

GLOUCESTER MASSACHUSETTS

ROCKPORT PUBLISHERS

CONTENTS

Introduction

The Incredible Impact of Lighting

Nothing has a greater impact on a space than lighting because illumination affects us on so many levels. Lighting influences the appearance, tone, and impression of every single object or space through how it is lighted. It can make or break the overall ambiance of any interior space.

Yet all too often, people add it as an afterthought—"Oh yes, let's also do some lighting"—after the architecture has been laid out and construction has begun. This is a huge mistake. Along with all the other design components, lighting needs to be considered at the beginning of the design process. Anyone taking on an interior project needs to learn at least the basics about lighting design so they can contribute to important decisions about lighting. Unfortunately, too many architects, interior designers, and contractors have had little training in this specialty.

Many new technologies have emerged during the past decade, making knowing the fundamentals of lighting design more necessary than ever. Who needed lighting expertise when the only thing available was a ceiling socket and a light bulb? Today, however, the range of choices is tremendous and presents a variety of luminaries (a "luminaire" is a complete fixture, including all parts necessary for positioning and obtaining power supply). Fluorescent lighting alone has gone through a revolutionary shift, and, with energy considerations and construction codes, it is a now a must for any space.

The Functions of Illumination

When planning lighting, focus on layering various types of lighting to accommodate the three elements that need illumination: people, architecture, and key objects such as art and collectibles. While all of these elements are important, the most critical consideration is lighting the people who will use the space.

Ambient: Soft General Illumination to Humanize a Space
Ambient lighting fills a room with a gentle, inviting overall glow that humanizes the space. To create good fill light, modern lighting design bounces illumination off walls and ceilings so the lighting is sensed only after being reflected. Thus glare and bright spots are avoided, and the light is flattering because it doesn't cast harsh shadows on people's faces. Ambient lighting may come from wall sconces, torchieres, or uplights mounted over cabinets, columns, or beams.

Decorative: Luminaires That Create Sparkle
The job of decorative luminaries, such as chandeliers, lanterns, and candlestick-type wall brackets, is to add shimmering texture and give the illusion of providing the room's ambient illumination. However, this type of lighting must be supported by a well-designed layer of supplementary lighting since decorative luminaries cannot be the source of overall illumination without overpowering the space.

Accent: Lighting That Highlights
Accent lighting uses carefully focused beams to illuminate an object, artwork, planting, or architectural detail. Artistic effect is a primary goal. Often, accent lighting is designed to make the viewer think the illumination is provided by a source that really does not provide much lighting at all, such as a candle or chandelier. Accent lighting can be provided by recessed adjustable luminaries, track lighting, or portable luminaries.

Task: Fixtures Geared for Work
Task lighting is the tightly focused, unobstructed, intense light needed where people do work or other activities requiring close scrutiny. Task lighting generally is provided by such luminaries as pharmacy-style lamps, tabletop lamps, undercabinet strip lighting, or, in bathrooms, as vertical strip light flanking the mirrors.

RESIDENTIAL SPACES

ENTRANCES

PORTALS TO THE HEART OF A HOME

Just as you judge a person by your first impression, you judge a home by what you see and sense at the entry.

As guests approach a house in the evening, outside lighting should create a welcoming impression. The house number should be lit, and cues indicating which way to approach and enter should be provided.

Inside the home, create an inviting atmosphere by layering the light. First, infuse the entry with ambient illumination. Fill light is especially important in this area, since gentle illumination helps people feel at ease in a new setting. Make sure the walls and ceiling aren't too dark for indirect light to be reflected and diffused effectively throughout the space.

Avoid the common error of relying on only one source of entrance illumination such as a decorative luminaire centered on the ceiling. A chandelier, for instance, will draw all the attention and

overpower the space. As you greet guests, you will end up in silhouette. Instead, install a good source of ambient light so that a chandelier can be dimmed to a subtle sparkle.

Naturally, accent lighting also should be part of the design. Using spots of illumination to highlight a dramatic painting, sculpture, or architectural detail can arouse guests' anticipation of what's to come as they explore the rest of the house.

Creating Illusion Through Lighting

Entrances come in all shapes and sizes, but by using lighting and

related design techniques you can redefine the envelope of the space. First, decide on your desired outcome. Do you want the entrance to look larger or more intimate? Do you want it to dazzle or to exude homey comfort?

If your entrance area is cramped, for example, you may be able to use illusion and lighting to visually "steal" an area of another room and make it seem part of the entrance. Directing accent lighting onto a sculpture, flower arrangement, or painting visible in an adjacent room helps make that area seem part of the entry. Techniques utilizing mirrors and glass blocks also can make entrances seem larger. If the entrance illumination does not adequately light the ceiling, it

The chandelier in this grand entry is dimmed to a glow, while recessed fixtures focus on the art and flowers.

Lighting and Interior Design: J. Hettinger Interiors
Architecture: Barry Holloway
Photo: Doug Johnson

not only makes the room seem small but neglects what often can be wonderful decorative elements in a design. Beams, coffers, moldings, ceiling frescoes, and other well-lit design components can become marvelous details, visually expanding the space upward and giving people something to engage their interest as they enter. When illuminated, stairways in an entrance also make the area seem larger and provide another focus for guests' attention. Lighting a painting on the stairway wall, or plants or sculpture on a stair landing, also helps a small entry assume the appearance of a grander entrance hall.

(Overleaf) Cove lighting is integrated into the architectural detail of the house. Recessed downlights emphasize the columns.

Lighting and Interior Design: J. Hettinger Interiors
Photo: Doug Johnson

The well-proportioned entry invites people to the windows and the sea beyond. Uplighting of the structural beams adds a sense of solidity.

Lighting Design and Architecture: Lucky Bennett
Interior Design: Peggy Chestnut
Photo: Russell Abraham

A series of torch-like wall sconces mounted on the wood beams invite guests into the various rooms off the entrance.

Lighting Design: Randall Whitehead, IALD,
　and Catherine Ng, IES
Interior Design: Carol Saal
Architecture: Stan Field
Photo: Dennis Anderson

The shaded chandelier and candlestick wall sconces seem to provide all the room's illumination. In reality, the Roman bust and console table are highlighted with miniature recessed adjustable fixtures made especially for remodeling projects.

Lighting Design: Randall Whitehead, IALD,
　and Catherine Ng, IES
Interior Design: Christian Wright
Photo: Dennis Anderson

A copper luminaire swoops down from the ceiling to provide accent lighting through a sculptural medium.

Lighting Design:
　Randall Whitehead, IALD,
　and Catherine Ng, IES
Interior Design: Carol Saal
Architecture: Stan Field
Photo: Dennis Anderson

A recessed framing projector casts an intriguing pattern of light onto the fluted wall detail. A pair of recessed low-voltage fixtures bounces light off the ball-capped newel post.

Lighting Design: Craig Roeder, IALD
Interior Design: Loyd Ray Taylor and Charles Paxton Gremillion
Photo: Robert Ames Cook

A mirror ball tucked behind the cap of the carved chest adds a touch of theater to this entryway.

Lighting Design: Randall Whitehead, IALD,
　and Catherine Ng, IES
Interior Design: Randall Whitehead
Photo: Dennis Anderson

Well lighting mounted in the floor at the base of the two pedestals casts intricate shadows onto the vaulted ceiling.

Lighting Design: Craig Roeder, IALD
Interior Design: Loyd Ray Taylor and Charles Paxton Gremillion
Architecture: Hendricks & Wall
Photo: Robert Ames Cook

The refraction off the clock onto the wall adds an amazing multidimensionality to this entrance hall. Uplights softly highlight the architectural detailing of the columns and a chest that once belonged to Marie Antoinette.

Lighting Design: Craig Roeder, IALD
Interior Design: Loyd Ray Taylor and Charles Paxton Gremillion
Architecture: Hendricks & Wall
Photo: Robert Ames Cook

Indirect lighting along the circumference of the dome detail highlights the silver leaf finish. Recessed low-voltage luminaires add visual interest to the center table and clock.

Lighting Design: Barbara Bouyea, IALD, IES
Interior Design and Architecture: Mil Bodron
Photo: Ira Montgomery

Cove lighting along this incredible entry's coffered ceiling keeps the architectural detailing from being lost. The magnificent chandelier hides an indirect halogen source that brings the crystals to life and provides additional ambient light.

Lighting Design:
  Barbara Bouyea, IALD, IES
Interior Design:
  Bobbie Dawn Lander
Architecture:
  Richard Drummond Davis
Photo: Ira Montgomery

A pair of art-glass sconces flank this entrance area. Lighting in the living room draws the eye, with recessed adjustable luminaires accenting the coromandel screen and coffee table.

Lighting and Interior Design: McDonald & Moore, Ltd.
Architecture: Duncan Todd, AIA
Photo: David Livingston

Indirect lighting incorporated into corbel-like wall sconces illuminates the groin-vault ceiling. Recessed adjustable accent lighting focuses on the art and flowers.

Lighting Design: Barbara Bouyea, IALD, IES
Interior Design: Bobbie Dawn Lander
Architecture: Richard Drummond Davis
Photo: Ira Montgomery

The custom tabletop and pendant luminaires by Ahnalisa Moore lend an amber glow to the entrance's wood surfaces in this mountain home.

Lighting Design: Ahnalisa Moore
Interior Design: Maria Tenglia
Architecture: Gary Francis & Assoc.
Photo: Scott Zimmerman

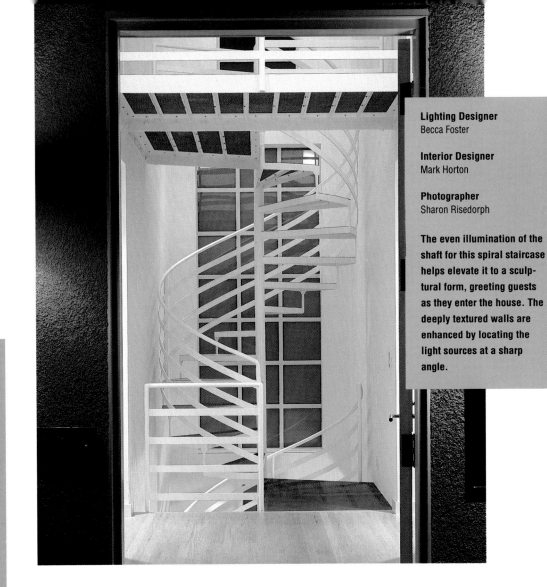

Lighting Designer
Becca Foster

Interior Designer
Mark Horton

Photographer
Sharon Risedorph

The even illumination of the shaft for this spiral staircase helps elevate it to a sculptural form, greeting guests as they enter the house. The deeply textured walls are enhanced by locating the light sources at a sharp angle.

Lighting Designer
Catherine Ng and
Randall Whitehead

Interior Designer
Lawrence Masnada

Architect
Sid Del Mar Leach

Photographer
Kenneth Rice

The almost surreal look of this illuminated railing is accomplished by using fiber optics mounted inside a channel routed into the underside of the Lucite. The owner can transform the color and feel of the entire railing simply by turning a color wheel located within the remote light source.

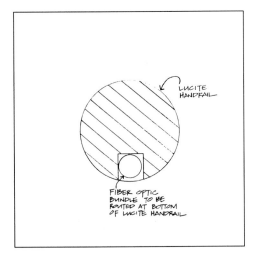

LUCITE HANDRAIL

FIBER OPTIC BUNDLE TO BE ROUTED AT BOTTOM OF LUCITE HANDRAIL

Lighting Designer
Claudia Librett

Interior Designer
Claudia Librett

Photographer
Durston Saylor

A combination of recessed fixtures and intra-beam uplighting helps add drama to this massive space.

Lighting Designer
Linda Ferry

Interior Designer
John Schneider

Photographer
Gil Edelstein

This downstairs corridor leading to the central foyer is illuminated by three spotted downlights creating a pattern that leads a visitor to the photograph and chest.

COMPACT FLUORESCENT FIXTURE

MOULDING

COLUMN

Lighting Designer
Randall Whitehead

Interior Designer
Jessica Hall and Joanne McDowell

Photographer
Christopher Irion

The warm amber light above the columns is, amazingly, a compact fluorescent source. Fluorescent sources come in hundreds of colors now.

Lighting Designer
Linda Ferry

Interior Designer
John Schneider

Photographer
Gil Edelstein

A twenty-foot long entry bridge with glass and beam roof utilizes four light sources, including incandescent mini strip light fixtures routed into the top of these beams which are carefully concealed to avoid reflection in the multiple glass surfaces and create an impressive uplighting effect.

Lighting Designer
Charles J. Grebmeier
and Gunnar Burklund

Interior Designer
Charles J. Grebmeier
and Gunnar Burklund

Photographer
Eric Zepeda

**Day and night shots show
how light can affect a
space.**

Lighting Designer
Randall Whitehead
and Catherine Ng

Interior Designer
Christian Wright and
Gerald Simpkins

Photographer
Ben Janken

**The 3-foot-wide hall was
made to seem visually large
by mirroring between three
shallow columns. The**
**original candlestick-type
wall brackets were
removed and wall
sconces, mimicking the
ziggurat details of the
architecture, became
"winged capitols."
Several recessed
adjustable fixtures light
the hallway and art,
while the glass block is
illuminated by fill light in
the kitchen beyond.**

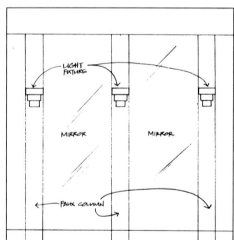

Lighting Designer
Randall Whitehead

Interior Designer
Christian Wright and
Gerald Simpkins

Photographer
Randall Whitehead

**A 20-watt halogen track
fixture brings out the form
and colors of this sculptural
flower arrangement.**

Lighting Designer
Kenton Knapp and
Robert Truax

Interior Designer
Charles Falls

Photographer
Mary Nichols

**Recessed adjustable
fixtures breathe life into the
art as metal wall sconces
show off the ceiling
details.**

Lighting Designer
Becca Foster

Interior Designer
Joseph Michalsky

Photographer
Philip Pavliger

**This detail shot of the entry
shows how dramatic and
special a space can
become with the use of
well-placed lighting. A pair
of downlights brings out the
color and texture of the
weaving and the spectacular
flower arrangement.**

Lighting Designer
Kenton Knapp and
Robert Truax

Interior Designer
Charles Falls and
Kenton Knapp

Photographer
Eric Zepeda

**Lowered fixtures emphasize
the relief of gilded carvings
and the coloration of the oriental screen, as a torchlike
wall sconce fills the area
with a pleasing illumination.**

Lighting Designer
David Story

Interior Designer
Dorian Muncey

Photographer
David Story

This grand entrance seems to invite people to waltz around the gray and white marble floor. Recessed downlights and wall sconces (not shown from this angle) bathe the walls and columns in a butter-yellow light as if the room were being illuminated by a roaring fire.

Lighting Designer
David Story

Interior Designer
Dorian Muncey

Photographer
David Story

The incredible ceiling height of this entry is brought down to a more human scale with the addition of a grand chandelier. The room's real illumination comes from the recessed downlights and wall sconces so that the chandelier can be dimmed to a soft sparkle.

Lighting Designer
Nan Rosenblatt

Interior Designer
Nan Rosenblatt

Photographer
Russell Abraham

Two recessed adjustable fixtures highlight a floral painting while incandescent mini strip light fixtures, hidden behind the perimeter, illuminate the domed ceiling detail.

Lighting Designer
Kenton Knapp and
Robert Truax

Interior Designer
Charles Falls

Photographer
Mary Nichols

Well-placed lighting helps the exterior become part of the interior space.

Lighting Designer
Randall Whitehead

Interior Designer
Lawrence Masnada

Photographer
John Benson

The dark-colored surfaces of the entry recede into the background allowing the large tropical arrangement to take prominence. The recessed adjustable fixtures provide the accent light for the flowers and pick up the white floor tiles.

Lighting Designer
Susan Huey, James Benya, Brian Fogerty and Ross De Alessi

Photographer
Douglas Salin

Lalique illuminated from underneath uses low-voltage iris projectors.

LIVING ROOMS
BLENDING DRAMA WITH VERSATILITY

In the past, living rooms seemed to be off limits except when entertaining company. Nowadays, though, living rooms aren't just reserved for special occasions. As the old "hands-off" formality softens, living room furniture is becoming more comfortable, its arrangement more relaxed. Furniture plans also are less static, with decorative items rotated around the house to keep the look fresh. Thus lighting should be as flexible as the rest of the home's components, and it needs to satisfy a variety of needs. Lighting for entertaining in the living room is important, but your main concern should be adequate illumination for day-to-day activities.

Overall Lighting

The first way to make your living room more inviting is to provide adequate ambient light. Perhaps the easiest alternative is flanking the fireplace with torchieres. A better solution–one that provides illumination that's more even–is four wall sconces.

If your living room has a 9-foot (2.7-meter) or higher ceiling, you have additional options. Pendant luminaires with an overall length of 2 to 2 1/2 feet (.6 to .8 meters) work well for a 9- to 12-foot-high (2.7- to 3.7-meter-high) flat ceiling. Pitched ceilings require luminaires adapted for the slope.

A higher ceiling also works well in conjunction with cove lighting, where the light source is hidden behind a crown molding or valence. In living rooms with gabled ceilings and support beams parallel to the floor, linear strip lighting can be mounted on top of the beams to create ambient light.

Focusing Light for Effect

Once fill light is provided, the next consideration is accent lighting. Remember that the type of luminaire chosen for accent lighting should be flexible. As you move furniture and art, the lighting needs to be able to accommodate new arrangements.

Recessed Lighting   Recessed adjustable luminaires are excellent for accent lighting. In new construction and remodeling projects, think about possible furniture arrangements before designing the lighting, since placement depends on what might be highlighted. In an existing residence that already has recessed luminaires, you can increase

flexibility by leaving the housing (the main part of a recessed luminaire installed inside the ceiling) and replacing the trim (the visible part of a recessed unit, attached to the housing) with line- or low-voltage adjustable versions.

Track Lighting   Use track lighting when other options aren't available. For example, if the ceiling depth is inadequate for housing recessed luminaires, then a surface-mounted system must be used. In living rooms, track lighting works best in a perimeter run. Installing molding on either side of the track helps integrate the system with the architecture.

Halogen Bridge Systems   An alternative to recessed and track lighting is a relatively new product, generically called a halogen bridge or cable system. This low-voltage setup runs two parallel wires across a ceiling space. Accent luminaires are then clipped and locked into place along the wires.

Task Lighting

Finally, plan the task lighting. Think about what you'll be doing in the living room, from reading to watching television to playing cards or board games. If you're building a new house and want to place furniture in the middle of the room, remember to specify floor plugs so cords don't cross the floor to a wall outlet.

A whimsical wall sconce provides a glow of warm light, while recessed, adjustable, low-voltage fixtures gently highlight the tablescape.

Lighting Design: Randall
   Whitehead, IALD, ASID
   Affiliate and Catherine Ng,
   IES
Interior Design: Jessica Hall &
   Associates
Photo: Dennis Anderson

(Overleaf) Recessed adjustable low-voltage luminaires illuminate the many fine art objects in this richly detailed Dallas residence. The highly adjustable system allows lights to be repositioned when items are moved to new locations.

Lighting Design: Craig Roeder, IALD
Interior Design: Loyd Ray Taylor and
   Charles Paxton Gremillion
Photo: Robert Ames Cook

*Recessed small-aperature fixtures subtly highlight the art
and tabletops, allowing the candles to give the illusion of
providing the illumination.*

Lighting Design: Randall Whitehead, IALD, ASID Affiliate
    and Catherine Ng, IES
Interior Design: Jessica Hall & Associates
Photo: Dennis Anderson

*Recessed accent lights make a dramatic statement for a
pair of sitting Buddha figures.*

Lighting Design: Randall Whitehead, IALD, ASID Affiliate
    and Catherine Ng, IES
Interior Design: Jessica Hall & Associates
Photo: Dennis Anderson

Recessed adjustable fixtures with mirror reflectors

accent the art in the room. Uplighting behind the palm

casts graceful shadows on the ceiling.

Lighting Design: Linda Ferry, IES, ASID Affiliate
Interior Design: John Schneider
Architecture: William David Martin, AIA
Photo: Douglas A. Salin

Recessed fixtures mounted alongside the skylight

create an island of light in the seating area. Track

fixtures accent art and plants.

Lighting Design: Linda Ferry, IES, ASID Affiliate
Architecture: David Allen Smith
Photo: Douglas A. Salin

Recessed adjustable low-voltage

luminaires set at an acute angle

bring out the texture of the stone

wall, while well-hidden indirect

lighting enhances the wood ceiling.

Lighting Design: Linda Ferry, IES,
 ASID Affiliate
Interior Design:
 Winifred Dell'Ario
Architecture:
 George Brook-Kothlow
Photo: Douglas A. Salin

The reading lamp's opaque copper shade projects light downward, keeping the brightness from interfering with the room's overall ambiance.

A handcrafted pendant fixture by Christina Spann helps set the mood in this Tuscany-style living room. Indirect cove lighting shows off the ceiling detail while adding ambient light. Exterior lighting visually opens up the room.

Lighting Design: Catherine Ng, IES, and
  Randall Whitehead, IALD, ASID Affiliate
Interior Design: Jessica Hall & Associates
Photo: Dennis Anderson

Display niches on either side of the fireplace use 50-watt halogen recessed fixtures to show off treasures.

In a residence done in Mediterranean Spanish style, the open-beam ceiling made the living room seem dark and oppressive. The solution: custom-designed sconces that humanize the space by creating a secondary ceiling line, and low-profile track fixtures by Capri that illuminate the palms and coffee table.

Lighting Design: Linda Ferry, IES, ASID Affiliate
Interior Design: Dudley Williams
Architecture: Rollen E. Stringham
Photo: Douglas A. Salin

Indirect lighting along the side walls adds a subtle glow to the sloped ceiling. A few well-placed monopoint luminaires highlight the table.

Lighting and Interior Design:
    Lindy Smallwood
Photo: Doug Johnson

Indirect cove lighting and recessed adjustable fixtures

work together to create a cohesive, comfortable

environment.

Lighting and Interior Design: J. Hettinger Interiors
Photo: Doug Johnson

This very traditional setting uses just a few recessed fixtures to accent the tapestry, allowing the wall sconces and table lamps to appear to be the room's sources of illumination.

Lighting Design: Alfredo Zaparolli
Interior Design: Eugene Anthony
Photo: John Vaughan

At night, well-placed fixtures illuminate the living room of this mountain retreat. A flexible system tucked between the beams provides accent lighting, while the warm glow of the mica table lamp and roaring fire invite people in.

Lighting and Interior Design: William David Martin
Photo: Douglas A. Salin

Recessed adjustable fixtures highlight the coromandel screen, art, and flowers. Table lamps add an intimate ambiance without overpowering the surroundings.

Lighting and Interior Design:
Donald Maxcy, ASID
Photo: Russell Abraham

Lighting Designer
Claudia Librett

Interior Designer
Claudia Librett

Photographer
Durston Saylor

The interaction of light and shadow add a great deal of interest to this living space. The low-voltage PAR36 fixtures highlight various objects while the wall sconces provide the necessary ambient light.

Lighting Designer
Ross De Alessi and Brian Fogerty

Interior Designer
George Saxe and Ted Cohen

Photographer
Ross De Alessi

Art turns this living room into an enchanted gallery.

Lighting Designer
Linda Ferry

Interior Designer
Michelle Pheasant

Photographer
Gil Edelstein

A flexible light plan accommodates the functions of each room and still gives a unified sense to the interior.

Lighting Designer
Donald Maxcy

Interior Designer
William Reno

Photographer
Russell Abraham

A display case becomes the focal point in this room with the use of well-concealed incandescent mini-strip lights. Multiple recessed adjustable fixtures bring other objects into focus.

Lighting Designer
Linda Esselstein

Interior Designer
Sharon Marston

Photographer
Russell Abraham

A simple low-voltage system adds dramatic emphasis to this living room. The marble fireplace is almost art in itself while the two bisque urns stand guard.

Lighting Designer
Randall Whitehead

Interior Designer
Lawrence Masnada

Photographer
Cecile Keefe

The lighting, when dimmed to a low level, bathes this San Francisco living room in a radiant glow of amber light. The walls are washed with illumination coming from behind a valance detail that surrounds the entire room.

Lighting Designer
Linda Ferry

Interior Designer
David Allen Smith

Photographer
Douglas Salin

A low-voltage wire system acts as both sculpture and a source of accent lighting while the halogen pendant fixture adds fill light to the space and highlights the bowl of fruit on the table.

Lighting Designer
Linda Ferry

Interior Designer
John Schneider

Photographer
Gil Edelstein

In this study, two concrete wall sconces add a soft background light to balance out the room with the addition of accents on the bookcases using recessed wall washers.

Lighting Designer
Ruth Soforenko

Interior Designer
Ruth Soforenko

Photographer
Russell Abraham

Track fixtures add dramatic highlights to this living room.

Lighting Designer
Randall Whitehead

Interior Designer
Christian Wright and
Gerald Simpkins

Photographer
Randall Whitehead

A blue filter enhances the
color of this vase.

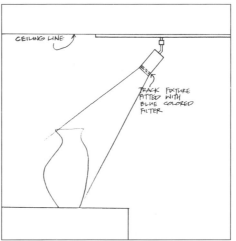

CEILING LINE

TRACK FIXTURE
FITTED WITH
BLUE COLORED
FILTER

Lighting Designer
James Benya

Interior Designer
Sharon Marston

Photographer
John Vaughan

This dynamic living room is
intriguing and exciting at the
same time. The brass and
black torchieres provide a
calming ambient light while
low-voltage fixtures highlight the table and screens.
Light passing through the
plant branches projects
shadows onto the adjoining
wall.

Lighting Designer
Kenton Knapp and Robert Truax

Interior Designer
Charles Falls

Photographer
Eric Zepeda

Each shelf is individually
illuminated to create this
stunning space.

Lighting Designer
Charles J. Grebmeier and
Gunnar Burklund

Interior Designer
Charles J. Grebmeier and
Gunnar Burklund

Photographer
Eric Zepeda

This room has twelve
different sources of light,
not including candlelight,
most of which are small
and not noticeable.

Lighting Designer
Jeffrey Werner

Interior Designer
Jeffrey Werner

Photographer
David Livingston

Warmth and intimacy
welcome a visitor to this
comforting living room
through the soft tones and
fireplace.

Lighting Designer
Randall Whitehead

Interior Designer
Eugene Anthony

Photographer
Christopher Irion

Lighting brings out the
elegance in this superb
living room adding to the
lushness of the furnishings.

Lighting Designer
Randall Whitehead

Interior Designer
Lawrence Masnada

Photographer
Jeremiah O. Bragstad

This intimate living room corner holds the game table. A flexible light fixture, mounted in between the windows, provides good shadowless light for card playing and makes a great display light for the orchid.

FLEXIBLE LIGHT
FIXTURE

GAME TABLE

Lighting Designer
Jeffrey Werner

Interior Designer
Jeffrey Werner

Photographer
David Livingston

This intriguing bronze sculpture is subtly illuminated from the front as a fountain of gas flame glows behind it.

Lighting Designer
Michael Souter

Interior Designer
Michael Souter

Photographer
Ross De Alessi

A sculptural 12-volt system supplies an artistic source of accent lighting.

Lighting Designer
Charles J. Grebmeier
and Gunnar Burklund

Interior Designer
Charles J. Grebmeier
and Gunnar Burklund

Photographer
Eric Zepeda

A tabletop arrangement shows how candlelight is still an important lighting element. The view is enhanced by a well-illuminated church steeple.

DINING ROOMS

THE MOVEABLE FEAST

Geared for sit-down entertaining for moderate to large groups, dining rooms used to be the last holdout for a traditional static furniture arrangement. After realizing how little time actually was spent formally entertaining at that big table, though, many homeowners have claimed this underutilized room for additional purposes.

To that end, dining room tables have become more flexible in size, folding down to provide more intimate seating for four, or dividing to make a pair of game tables. Even people who still have a large table want to be able to occasionally push it against a wall for buffet dining. All of these changes have set up a need for adjustable lighting and forced homeowners and designers to rethink traditional dining room lighting.

Chandelier Alternatives and Solutions

For eons, the dining room table has been perfectly centered under a chandelier. Now that tables are

moved around, though, centered chandeliers tend to get in the way. Some people who aren't tied to a traditional approach turn to recessed adjustable lighting to provide illumination for the table. For instance, three recessed adjustable luminaires can be used. The middle one highlights the centerpiece. The two outside luminaires cross-illuminate the tabletop itself, adding sparkle to the dishes and silverware. (Make sure the outside luminaires don't point straight down, which would cast harsh shadows on diners and create tabletop glare.) Many homeowners, however, still prefer a chandelier above the table. If you want the flexibility to rearrange furniture but also want traditional lighting, consider the following options:

- Use decorative lighting that hugs the ceiling so the luminaire doesn't look odd when the table is moved.
- Select a pendant light on a pulley system that raises or lowers the luminaire.
- Hang a crystal-type chandelier in a recessed dome so the luminaire's visual relationship is linked to the ceiling configuration rather than the table location.

Getting That Overall Glow

Whichever option you choose for table illumination, don't forget that ambient light also is needed. Torchieres or wall sconces can do the trick. If the dining room has a dome detail, the perimeter can be illuminated so fill light bounces off

the dome's interior. Cove lighting is another excellent source of ambient light. To successfully light a cove, install an even and continuous line of light, preferably from 12- or 24-volt incandescent light rails.

Accenting with Light

If you prefer a traditional dining room chandelier setup, consider adding a recessed adjustable light on either side to add drama to the table. This provides accent lighting for the tabletop and its centerpiece, and also allows the chandelier to be dimmed to a glittering glow while giving the impression of providing the table's illumination. Next, think about lighting for the walls. Instead of illuminating every piece of wall art, allow some items to fall into secondary importance, so they gradually can be discovered by guests. And don't forget to add one or two recessed adjustable luminaires to spotlight the side table, buffet, or console area.

(Overleaf) The sloped ceiling is emphasized by a run of linear low-voltage lighting hidden within the cove detail. Track fixtures highlight the table.

Lighting Design: Linda Ferry,
    IES, ASID Affiliate
Interior Design: John Newcomb
Architecture: Stephen Wilmot
Photo: Douglas A. Salin

A chandelier and perforated metal, fan-shaped wall sconce add romance to this intimate dining room, and recessed adjustable fixtures illuminate the art and tabletop.

Lighting Design: Randall
    Whitehead, IALD, ASID
    Affiliate and Catherine Ng, IES
Interior Design: Jessica Hall &
    Associates
Photo: J. D. Peterson

Recessed adjustable fixtures add

style to a peaceful dining

experience. Exterior lighting

throws an intriguing shadow

pattern on the wall. Votive

candles cast a golden glow that

adds to the ambience (left).

Lighting Design: Catherine Ng,
    IES, and Randall Whitehead,
    IALD, ASID Affiliate
Interior Design: Jessica Hall &
    Associates
Photo: Dennis Anderson

Contemporary luminaires often blend artistic design with function, as is the case with this opaque pendant by Lightspann and the Mirano glass torchiere.

Lighting and Interior Design:
    Sherry Scott
Photo: John Martin

Recessed adjustable downlights contribute to this dazzling dining room tableau. Votive candles add sparkle without use of a chandelier, while sconces such as the one to the right of the fireplace provide fill light.

Lighting/Interior Design and
    Architecture: Gordon Stein
Photo: Douglas A. Salin

The grouping of cone-shaped pendants becomes a sculptural entity off the dining room table. Wall sconces provide ambient light, while recessed downlights guide people from room to room.

Lighting and Interior Design: Carla Carstens, ASID, CID
Architecture: Michael Helm
Photo: Douglas A. Salin

Fantasy and function blend together to create this intriguing vignette. A circular metal framework supports swags of richly textured fabric as well as the lighting that illuminates the table and art objects.

Lighting Design: Terry Ohm
Interior Design: Bob Miller
Photo: Douglas A. Salin

Lighting within the casework highlights a collection of stemware. Recessed adjustable fixtures are an important aspect of the lighting plan.

Lighting Design: Michael Souter,
  IALD, ASID
Interior Design: Bob Miller,
  Flegels
Photo: Douglas A. Salin

Recessed adjustable low-voltage luminaires draw

attention to the art and tabletop.

Lighting Design: Donald Maxcy, ASID
Interior Design: Bill Reno
Photo: Russell Abraham

Monopoint track fixtures mounted on the side of the

beams illuminate the tabletops. Noguchi lanterns help

humanize the space's scale.

Lighting and Interior Design: Donald Maxcy, ASID
Architecture: Fletcher & Hardoin
Photo: Ron Starr

Recessed downlights illuminate the walls and chandelier of this dining room, while large palms flanking the entrance fall into silhouette.

Lighting and Interior Design: J. Hettinger Interiors
Photo: Doug Johnson

The magnificent sailing ship chandelier gives the illusion of providing the room's illumination, but recessed fixtures actually do the job of highlighting the art and tabletop.

Lighting Design: Linda Ferry, IES, ASID Affiliate
Interior Design: Valera W. Lyles
Photo: Douglas A. Salin

This modern dining room uses wall sconces of forged metal and blown glass to provide ambient illumination. Indirect lighting above the partial wall adds yet another dimension.

Lighting Design: Dahlin Group
Photo: Doug Johnson

A sculptural halogen wire system illuminates the Japanese-style dining area. Recessed adjustable fixtures highlight the owner's collection of art and ceramics.

Lighting and Interior Design: Don Maxcy, ASID
Photo: Russell Abraham

A wonderful grouping of candles and old-style light fixtures adds romance to this dining room. A single recessed accent light highlights the arrangement of spring branches.

Lighting Design: Randall Whitehead, IALD, and
    Catherine Ng, IES
Interior Design: Christian Wright
Photo: Dennis Anderson

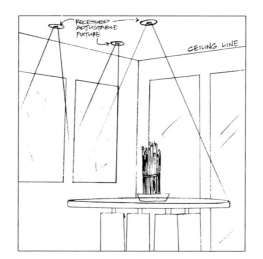

Lighting Designer
Randall Whitehead
and Catherine Ng

Interior Designer
Christian Wright and
Gerald Simpkins

Photographer
Ben Janken

This small dining room
(8' x 10') seems larger
because the deck beyond is
illuminated so that visually
it becomes part of the
interior space. Recessed
adjustable fixtures
highlight the floral
arrangement on the table
and the paintings. The
addition of a daylight blue
filter helps keep the colors
of the artwork crisp.

Lighting Designer
Linda Ferry

Interior Designer
John Schneider

Photographer
Gil Edelstein

A dramatic backlight helps
draw the eye. This partition
between the living room
and the dining room is used
as an art wall to limit the
focus to the dining area.

Lighting Designer
Randall Whitehead
and Catherine Ng

Interior Designer
Christian Wright and
Gerald Simpkins

Photographer
Ben Janken

Here, many lighting techniques blend together to create this inviting environment. Wall sconces using soft pink bulbs provide an ambient light that is complimentary to skin tones. The recessed accent lights fitted with daylight blue filters give a crisp, white illumination to the art. The exterior lights also are fitted with daylight blue filters to keep the plants looking lush and green. The balance of light inside and out keeps the windows from becoming black mirrors at night.

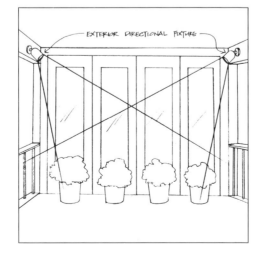

EXTERIOR DIRECTIONAL FIXTURE

Lighting Designer
Charles J. Grebmeier and
Gunnar Burklund

Interior Designer
Charles J. Grebmeier and
Gunnar Burklund

Photographer
Eric Zepeda

The bookcase in this dining
room creates a great deal of
warmth — especially since
there is no fireplace.

Lighting Designer
Kenton Knapp

Interior Designer
Charles Falls and Kenton
Knapp

Photographer
Patrick Barta

Incandescent mini strip
light fixtures add delicate
illumination to this ornate
ceiling detail and perimeter
recessed adjustable
fixtures highlight the
objects in the space.

Lighting Designer
Kenton Knapp

Interior Designer
Charles Falls and Kenton
Knapp

Photographer
Eric Zepeda

Miniature halogen wall
brackets bounce a rich fill
light off the cove ceiling
detail while recessed
fixtures punch up the
flower arrangement, plants,
silver service and wood
detailing.

Lighting Designer
Jeffrey Werner

Interior Designer
Jeffrey Werner

Photographer
David Livingston

Opportune lighting turns this dining room into a vibrant setting with a lush, well-lighted exterior landscape while recessed adjustable fixtures accent the table, painting, and counter.

Lighting Designer
Becca Foster

Interior Designer
Michael Harris

Photographer
John Martin

A halogen bridge system spans the dining room while a pair of recessed wall washer fixtures adds an even illumination to the hanging oriental screen.

Lighting Designer
Catherine Ng and
Randall Whitehead

Interior Designer
Lawrence Masnada

Architect
Sid Del Mar Leach

Photographer
Kenneth Rice

A custom-designed suspended ceiling detail completes a visual echo between the oval ceiling and the dining room table in this Twin Peaks residence in San Francisco. Recessed adjustable fixtures provide all the accent lighting as wall sconces and concealed cove lighting create the overall glow.

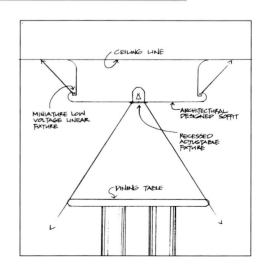

CEILING LINE

MINIATURE LOW
VOLTAGE LINEAR
FIXTURE

ARCHITECTURAL
DESIGNED SOFFIT

RECESSED
ADJUSTABLE
FIXTURE

DINING TABLE

Lighting Designer
James Benya

Interior Designer
Sharon Marston

Photographer
John Vaughan

Form and texture are highlighted in this setting. Recessed downlights graze the centerpiece and chairs, creating a perfect setting for conversations and dining.

Lighting Designer
Don Maxcy

Interior Designer
Oliver White

Photographer
Russell Abraham

A custom lighting slot in the ceiling accents the flower arrangement on the table and other objects in the space, while uplighting casts dappled shadows on the sloped surfaces.

Lighting Designer
James Benya and Deborah Witte

Interior Designer
Karen Carroll

Photographer
James Benya

Recessed adjustable fixtures do the work while the chandelier provides the elegance.

Lighting Designer
Randall Whitehead
and Catherine Ng

Interior Designer
Linda Bradshaw-Allen

Photographer
Ben Janken

Halogen wall sconces with integral asymmetric reflectors throw light out into the room. These fixtures act like floating capitals for the columns on the long wall. The window-like insets are uplighted with linear incandescent fixtures recessed below the sill line.

Lighting Designer
Randall Whitehead
and Catherine Ng

Interior Designer
Linda Bradshaw-Allen

Photographer
Ben Janken

The asymmetric reflectors inside the wall sconces mounted on the opposite wall throw a good amount of light on this side of the room. They allow the use of fewer fixtures to provide the necessary fill light that helps humanize the space. The French doors open onto a lagoon in Belvedere, California.

Lighting Designer
Kenton Knapp

Interior Designer
Charles Falls and
Kenton Knapp

Photographer
Mary Nichols

A lighting system was developed that incorporated the ambient light into the architectural detailing. The warm hue of the light plays up the colors used in the rooms. The open plan of the house allows family and guests to travel from kitchen to breakfast room to family room. The gentle-quality light helps to support this open feeling.

Lighting Designer
Robert Truax and Kenton Knapp

Interior Designer
Charles Falls

Photographer
Eric Zepeda

A cascade of flowers on the dining room table becomes a wonderful interplay of color and shadow through the use of recessed adjustable fixtures.

KITCHENS
TODAY'S GATHERING PLACE

The kitchen is the new center for entertaining, a preferred site for guests to congregate while the meal is being prepared. The reasons for this trend are many, from our culture's more relaxed attitudes, to the trend toward open-plan houses.

The impact on lighting is that today's kitchens should be as inviting as the rest of the house. Kitchens, too, must have controllable lighting levels, so that guests look good and feel comfortable. The color temperatures of the lamps should match, or at least be similar to, color temperatures in other areas of the house.

Sadly, many new kitchens – even very expensive ones – still are designed with only a single source of illumination in the center of the room. Whether incandescent or fluorescent, this luminaire essentially is a glare bomb that provides little in the way of adequate task, ambient, or accent

lighting. As the eye adjusts to the glare, the rest of the kitchen seems even darker than it is.

The same rule applies to lighting kitchens as other parts of the house: No single luminaire can perform all the functions of illumination at once. A layering of various light sources is essential. Many kitchen lighting solutions of past decades – the surface-mounted single luminaire, track lighting running down the ceiling center, a series of recessed downlights installed in a grid pattern – all present similar problems. They cast harsh unflattering shadows on

faces, and while performing kitchen tasks your own head eclipses the work surface. A well-thought-out lighting design, however, avoids these negatives.

Under-Cabinet Task Lighting

One key kitchen solution is lighting that is mounted below the upper cabinets which provides even illumination on the countertops. Since the lighting is between your head and the work surface, shadows are minimized. When planning, though, remember that placement is important. For instance, when fluorescent strip luminaires are mounted toward the back of the cabinet, the light can

hit diners sitting in the breakfast area right in the eye. A better alternative is linear incandescent or fluorescent task lights that mount toward the cabinet front. They project part of the illumination toward the backsplash, which then bounces onto the work surface and into the center of the kitchen. This works particularly well when the countertop surface is a non-specular material.

Spreading the Light

Many alternatives are available for ambient lighting. One possibility, if a kitchen has 9-foot (2.7-meter) ceilings or higher, is to install a series of opaque or translucent pendant-hung luminaires along the space's centerline. Not only will the pendants produce wonderful ambient illumination, but they also will add a more human scale to the kitchen.

Another popular option is installing fixtures above the cabinets to provide indirect lighting. Mount the fixtures flush with the cabinet front to prevent bright spots and to make sure displayed objects don't block the light. Add blocking that lifts decorative items to the fascia level, so they are not visually cut off at the bottom.

Highlighting Artwork

You might have a few art pieces that can stand up to an occasional splash of marinara sauce. Highlighting them helps make the kitchen blend into rest of the home. Once the party has moved to another area of an open-plan house, leaving on the accent lighting while dimming the kitchen's ambient and task lighting creates a tasty effect.

Recessed downlights offer task lighting at the sink area and add texture to the louvered shutters, while additional recessed adjustable fixtures focus on the art. An alabaster fixture brings fill light to the space.

Lighting and Interior Design:
  Donald Maxcy, ASID
Photo: Russell Abraham

(Overleaf) Translucent Mirano glass pendants do a terrific job of providing overall illumination for the kitchen. Recessed fixtures with black reflectors direct additional task light onto work surfaces, as do lights mounted below the upper cabinets.

Lighting Design:
  Randall Whitehead, IALD, ASID Affiliate, and
  Catherine Ng, IES
Interior Design: Toby Flax
Architecture: Teri Behm
Photo: Cesar Rubio

Low-voltage track fixtures mounted at the apex beam cross-illuminate the island's work surface. Indirect lighting adds fill light and enhances the architecture.

Lighting Design: Linda Ferry, IES, ASID Affiliate
Interior Design: John Newcomb
Architecture: Stephen Wilmot
Photo: Douglas A. Salin

The grid pattern above the kitchen hides adjustable task lighting, while under-cabinet lighting provides additional illumination for work.

Lighting Design: Linda Ferry, IES, ASID Affiliate
Architecture: David Allen Smith
Photo: Douglas A. Salin

This large, well-appointed kitchen opens into the

living and family room area. Pendant fixtures help

create a sense of separation between the various spaces.

Lighting and Interior Design: Catherine Ng, IES, and
    Randall Whitehead, IALD, ASID Affiliate
Interior Design: Jessica Hall & Associates
Photo: Dennis Anderson

Fill light comes from two pendant-hung indirect

fixtures. Black track heads illuminate the architectural

detail above the cabinets.

Lighting and Interior Design: Ace Architects
Architecture: Ace Architects
Photo: Russell Abraham

Spherical pendants provide task

lighting for the center island. A

combination direct and indirect

pendant fixture over the table

gives both fill and accent light.

Lighting Design:
    Michael Souter, IALD, ASID
Interior Design:
    Barbara Jacobs, ASID
Photo: Douglas A. Salin

Ribbed-glass pendants supply fill light along with some task lighting, and recessed downlights provide pathway light around the center island. The countertops are illuminated by under-cabinet linear halogen fixtures.

Lighting Design and Architecture: David Ludwig
Photo: Muffy Kibbey

Incandescent alabaster pendants and dimmable fluorescent-lensed downlights provide illumination for this upscale kitchen. Fixtures within the hood and below the upper cabinets offer good task lighting on the work surfaces.

Lighting Design:
    Randall Whitehead, IALD,
    ASID Affiliate,
    and Catherine Ng, IES
Interior Design: Diane Chapman
Architecture: Mark Thomas, AIA
Photo: Michael Bruk,
    Photo/Graphics

In this updated 1930s-style
kitchen, under-cabinet lighting
and recessed downlights
with regressed glass diffusers
flood the work surfaces with
illumination. A deco-influenced
center fixture dishes up the
necessary ambient light.

Lighting Design: Randall
    Whitehead, IALD, and
    Catherine Ng, IES
Interior Design: Christian Wright
Photo: Dennis Anderson

The most dramatic aspect of this kitchen's lighting design is the marble backsplash, which is illuminated from behind. Access to the luminaires is through the pantry, located on the other side of the wall. Under-cabinet fixtures and lighting within the cook-top hood provide excellent task light.

Lighting Design: David W. Patton
Photo: John Canham

The island in this cozy kitchen in a turn-of-the-century house is sparked by low-voltage pendants. The work areas are serviced by simple downlights and color-corrected fluorescent under-cabinet task lights.

Lighting Design:
    Ruth Soforenko, ASID,
    Debbie Collins, ASID
Interior Design:
    Ruth Soforenko, ASID
Photo: Russell Abraham

Indirect lighting within the skylight provides excellent

shadow-free task light for the kitchen, while keeping

the skylight from becoming a dark hole at night.

Lighting Design: Barbara Bouyea, IALD, IES
Interior Design: Cheri Etchelecu
Architecture: Bill Booziotis and Holly Hall
Photo: Ira Montgomery

This South American kitchen uses a triangular-shape
linear fluorescent fixture to play off the geometry of
the jet-age hood.

Lighting Design: Guinter Parschalk
Interior Design: Luiz Fernando Rocco
Architecture: Luiz Fernando Rocco/
    Vasco Andrade Lopes
Photo: Andres Otero

This kitchen's lighting (opposite and right) is fully
integrated as an architectural detail. Illumination
from clear alzak cone-aperture downlights provides
task lighting for the island and bounces off the
surface as ambient light. A concealed 24-volt light
rail above the curving soffit emphasizes the beauty of
the architectural form.

Lighting Design: Steven L. Klein, Standard Electric
    Supply Co.
Interior Design: Joanne Sheridan, Sturgeon Interiors, Ltd.
Architecture: Richard Sherer, Lakeside Development
Photo: Mark F. Heffron

Lighting Designer
Randall Whitehead
and Catherine Ng

Interior Designer
Christian Wright and
Gerald Simpkins

Photographer
Ben Janken

A custom gray granite
laminate facia was created
to hide linear task lighting
below these Euro-style
cabinets. In addition to
good task light, they
provide attractive accent
lighting for objects placed
on the counter.

Lighting Designer
Randall Whitehead
and Catherine Ng

Interior Designer
Chula Camp

Photographer
Ben Janken

This all-white kitchen
benefits from well-
concealed lighting under
the cabinets and pony wall
overhang. They provide a
good shadowless work
area. Halogen wall sconces
on the hallway wall (not
seen in this shot) provide
the fill light for this open
plan kitchen.

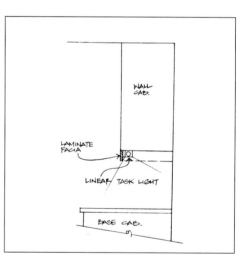

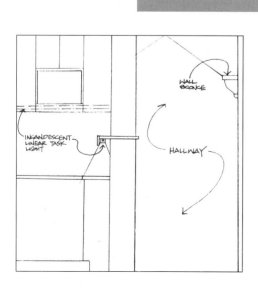

Lighting Designer
Claudia Librett

Interior Designer
Claudia Librett

Photographer
Durston Saylor

Soffit lighting in the kitchen washes the fronts of the cabinets with light while a reveal above creates a clean line of illumination.

Lighting Designer
Greg Smith

Interior Designer
Greg Smith

Photographer
Russell Abraham

Incandescent mini strip lights inside the hood give it a decidedly sculptural feeling. Track installed on the wall throws uplight onto the sloped ceiling.

Lighting Designer
Greg Smith

Interior Designer
William Reno

Photographer
Russell Abraham

The view from outside shows a creamy white kitchen. A soffit projects out over the counter and holds recessed adjustable fixtures that cast cones of illumination over the cabinet faces. Incandescent strip light fixtures provide good task light on the counter while a track run mounted on the wall throws light up along the ceiling.

Lighting Designer
Kenton Knapp and
Robert Truax

Interior Designer
Charles Falls

Photographer
Mary Nichols

This kitchen doubles as a futuristic art gallery with lighting as well integrated as the cabinetry.

Lighting Designer
Masahiko Uchiyama

Photographer
Toshitaka Niwa

Fixture designer Masahiko Uchiyama playfully combines the tools of the chef with light.

Lighting Designer
Osburn Design

Interior Designer
Osburn Design

Photographer
John Vaughan

Incandescent mini strip light fixtures inside the open cabinets subtly highlight this eclectic collection of cups and tins.

Lighting Designer
Osburn Design

Interior Designer
Osburn Design

Photographer
John Vaughan

Incandescent mini strip light fixtures hidden behind the crown moulding and range now provide a sunny illumination for this kitchen.

Lighting Designer
Becca Foster and Pam Morris

Interior Designer
Paul Vincent Wiseman
and Michael Harris

Photographer
John Martin

The gentle vault of the
ceiling is enhanced by the
diffuse light coming from
these 3 custom pendant-hung
fixtures. These fixtures, along
with fluorescent strip fixtures,
provide excellent shadowless
work light.

Lighting Designer
Jan Moyer

Interior Designer
Karen Libby

Photographer
Mary Nichols

The warm tones of this
striking wooden interior
come to life with indirect
light sources tucked above
beams and ceiling details.
Overscaled, spherelike
track fixtures light the
display case in the living
room area. A well-integrated
custom hanging fixture
above the kitchen island
provides both ambient and
task light.

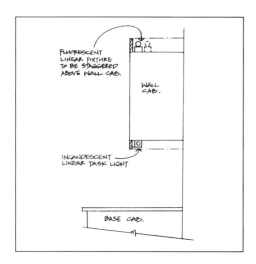

Lighting Designer
Becca Foster

Interior Designer
Mark Horton

Photographer
Sharon Risedorph

The crisp colors of this kitchen called for the use of color-corrected fluorescent sources. The intriguing use of desk lamps on the island gives wonderful, if unusual work light.

Lighting Designer
Randall Whitehead/
Catherine Ng

Interior Designer
Chula Camp

Photographer
David Livingston

Color-corrected fluorescent fixtures mounted above the cabinets along the perimeter of the kitchen provide an excellent fill light for the space. This allows the homeowners easy visibility inside the cupboards. Additional lighting below the cabinets gives a good shadowless work light on the counter-tops. Lighting in the pantry comes on automatically when the door is opened.

Lighting Designer
Randall Whitehead/
Catherine Ng

Interior Designer
Chula Camp

Photographer
David Livingston

The open plan of this kitchen and breakfast area is emphasized by the even

amount of fill light in the space. This illumination comes from strategically-placed wall sconces and fluorescent fixtures mounted above the cabinets (not shown from this angle). Recessed adjustable fixtures brighten up the table, the art work and the center island.

Lighting Designer
Jeffrey Werner

Interior Designer
Jeffrey Werner and Julie Hoefler

Photographer
David Livingston

A counter island surrounded by a gallery of art objects is further separated by a ceiling step-down detail that contains recessed downlights using halogen PAR bulbs.

Lighting Designer
Becca Foster

Interior Designer
Dianne Sugahara

Photographer
John Martin

This wonderful wood kitchen is enhanced by the use of incandescent sources. A white cone reflector in the recessed fixtures creates a wide spread of illumination to help reduce shadowing, while the hood over the stove pours light down onto the work surface.

Lighting Designer
Randall Whitehead

Interior Designer
Chula Camp

Photographer
Ben Janken

Adequate lighting above the cook-top is essential. The fixtures are called "jelly jars" because the bulb is encased in a jar-shaped glass casing to make cleanup easy and avoid a possible fire hazard.

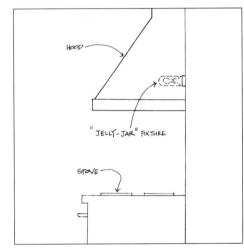

HOOD

"JELLY-JAR" FIXTURE

STOVE

Lighting Designer
Randall Whitehead
and Catherine Ng

Interior Designer
Chula Camp

Photographer
Ben Janken

This country French kitchen retains its charm by the use of incandescent lights mounted above and below the cabinetry. Recessed downlights illuminate the countertops that do not have overhead cupboards, and open skylights let in a pleasing, diffuse light.

Lighting Designer
Alfredo Zaparolli

Interior Designer
Rosemary Wilton

Photographer
Alfredo Zaparolli

The kitchen space is well-illuminated without overpowering the dining room area.

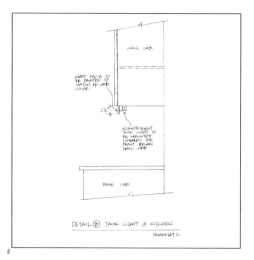

Lighting Designer
Becca Foster

Interior Designer
Dianne Sugahara

Photographer
John Martin

This fanciful mural helps get the creative cook's juices flowing. Recessed fixtures provide an area of illumination under the tree for the hard working Cupids.

Lighting Designer
Patricia Borba McDonald and Marcia Moore

Interior Designer
Patricia Borba McDonald and Marcia Moore

Photographer
Russell Abraham

Deep wood surfaces with polished brass accents are highlighted in this elegant kitchen emphasizing the warm finishes and maintaining a classical yet functional look throughout.

Bedrooms
A QUIET RETREAT

Often bedrooms are considered unimportant areas when lighting plans are put together. As a result, each bedroom gets stuck with a light in the center of the ceiling and a couple of bedside reading lamps.

But think about how much of the time we live in our bedrooms. We spend one-third of our lives sleeping, and countless more hours in the bedroom before and after sleep. When a bedroom is shared with a significant other, flattering light is particularly essential. After all, it's important to look your best in such an intimate setting.

Indirect Lighting

People are the main event in a bedroom setting. Help erase dark circles and soften age lines by providing adequate ambient light. Your partner will love you for it. If an existing luminaire is centered on the ceiling, an easy upgrade is to replace it with a pendant-hung

indirect light. This will provide illumination that bounces off the ceiling and walls to create shadow-free light. In houses with sloped ceilings, remember that the tall wall area above the door line doesn't have to be dead space. Mounting a series of two or three wall sconces there will create great fill light and not waste any art display wall space at normal viewing heights.

Cove lighting and other architectural solutions for creating ambient illumination often work beautifully in bedrooms. But if you're not ready to go that far, a pair of reasonably priced torchieres

will do the trick of throwing light on the ceiling. Also, you can place an indirect light source on top of a tall piece of furniture such as an armoire. A canopy bed with a solid top is another great location for hiding an indirect light.

Reading in Bed

In addition to ambient light, another function of illumination should be considered: task lighting for reading. If you choose the typical approach – portable luminaires (table lamps) on bedside tables – select shades with opaque liners. The liners will direct light down and across your reading matter, and also help keep the light from disturbing your bed mate.

Uplighting within the canopy emphasizes the bed, which is the room's focal point.

Lighting Design: Donald Maxcy, ASID
Interior Design: Bill Reno
Photo: Russell Abraham

Another possibility is installing wall-mounted swing-arm lamps, a flexible source of illumination that doesn't take up bedside table space. Mounting swing-arm lamps at the correct height is critical, however. To find the ideal height, get into bed and hunker down against the pillows in your normal reading position. Then measure from the floor to just above shoulder height. Why? Because the optimum spot to position task lighting is between the head and work surface. When loved ones sharing a bed nest in at different heights, compromises should be made on both sides so the reading lights can be mounted at matching heights.

(Overleaf) This table lamp is sophisticated but whimsical, combining great texture with simple geometry.

Lighting and Interior Design: April Sheldon, CID
Photo: John Casado

A recessed dome is uplighted using bendable linear low-voltage luminaires, giving the room a gentle overall glow.

Lighting Design: Axiom Design Inc.
Interior Design: Deborah Raye
Photo: Kenneth Rice

Two recessed adjustable fixtures above the bed provide

reading light, similar to the individual overhead lights

on airplanes.

Lighting and Interior Design: Donald Maxcy, ASID
Photo: Russell Abraham

The corner of this bedroom layers fill lighting from a

single torchiere with accent lighting from recessed

downlights over the window seat and in the bookcase.

Lighting and Interior Design: Donald Maxcy, ASID
Photo: Russell Abraham

Swing-arm lamps with opaque

metal shades offer excellent

reading light without glare.

Lighting and Interior Design:
Donald Maxcy, ASID
Photo: Russell Abraham

The sandblasted wall sconces and pendant by Johnson Art Studios lend a golden glow of illumination to this master bedroom in Sonoma, California.

Lighting Design: Randall Whitehead, IALD, ASID
    Affiliate, Catherine Ng, IES
Interior Design: Carol Saal
Architecture: Stan Field
Photo: Dennis Anderson

Beehive wall sconces by Phoenix Day Company flood light into this cool green sanctuary. A backlighted shoji panel provides a glimpse of the bonsai tree beyond, while recessed downlights show off the Chinese ceramics.

Lighting Design: Randall Whitehead, IALD, ASID
    Affiliate, and Catherine Ng, IES
Interior Design: Randall Whitehead
Photo: Dennis Anderson

A center opaque plaster pendant offers flattering ambient light, while dimmable bedside lamps provide illumination for reading.

Lighting Design: Randall Whitehead, IALD, ASID
    Affiliate, and Catherine Ng, IES
Interior Design: Christian Wright
Photo: Dennis Anderson

Inspired by a walk in the Tuileries in Paris, this flower lamp designed by April Sheldon has a base derived from some of the garden's architectural elements.

Lighting Design: April SHeldon, CID
Photo: John Casado

A row of miniature recessed downlights mounted within a soffit detail washes the wood paneling on the fireplace wall. A standing lamp with an opaque shade provides reading light without overpowering the space.

Lighting Design: Barbara Bouyea, IALD, IES
Interior Design and Architecture: Mil Bodron
Photo: Ira Montgomery

The intricately painted wall panels are evenly illuminated with a row of recessed wall-wash fixtures (opposite). Accent lights bring out the many gilded items in the room. Low-voltage recessed adjustable fixtures with black trims fade into the black ceiling (below), allowing elements of the room to be the primary focus.

Lighting Design: Craig Roeder, IALD
Interior Design: Loyd Ray Taylor and
    Charles Paxton Gremillion
Architecture: Hendricks & Wall
Photo: Robert Ames Cook

A lavender table lamp adds a luminous glow to

the seating area in this master bedroom suite.

The television in the console at the end of the bed

can easily be lowered when not in use.

Lighting and Interior Design: Kathy Monteiro
Photo: Doug Johnson

A deep soffit detail houses both accent and indirect

lighting in this spacious master bedroom.

Lighting Design: Craig Roeder, IALD
Interior Design: Duffala/von Thaden Assoc., Inc.
Architecture: Fleischman/Garcia Architects
Photo: Jeff Blankton

Wall sconces flank the bed in this child's room. A table

lamp with a perforated metal shade offers reading light

without glare.

Lighting Design: Catherine Ng, IES, and
    Randall Whitehead, IALD, ASID Affiliate
Interior Design: Joseph Ruggiero & Assoc.
Photo: Russell Abraham

Lighting Designer
Linda Ferry

Interior Designer
Carolyn Hardy

Photographer
Douglas Salin

The sumptuous bedroom benefits from the illuminated trees beyond the window. The bay window almost becomes a living screen and complements the one behind the bed.

Lighting Designer
Kenton Knapp and
Robert Truax

Interior Designer
Charles Falls

Photographer
Mary Nichols

A huge mineral stone appears to be glowing on the foreground coffee table.

Lighting Designer
Don Maxcy

Interior Designer
Don Maxcy

Photographer
Russell Abraham

A rounded cove detail provides a pleasing indirect light. Wall-mounted reading lights provide excellent illumination without glare.

Lighting Designer
Randall Whitehead and
Catherine Ng

Interior Designer
Christian Wright and
Gerald Simpkins

Photographer
Ben Janken

Glass block walls allow
light to travel from room to
room and help to get natural
ambient light into interior
rooms. Cantilevered wall
sconces throw light up and
out into the bedroom.

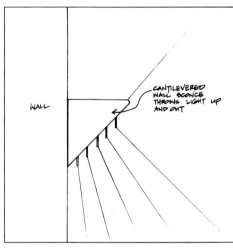

Lighting Designer
Pam Pennington

Interior Designer
Pam Pennington

Photographer
Russell Abraham

For a high-tech look on a
low budget, the existing
fixture in the center of the
room was replaced with
two suspended bars onto
which the designer
clamped low-voltage
fixtures fitted with curly cable.
A red filter projects
a fanciful spot of color on
the comforter.

Lighting Designer
Robert Truax and Kenton Knapp

Interior Designer
Charles Falls

Photographer
Eric Zepeda

Recessed adjustable
fixtures help create the
drama for this spectacular
penthouse bedroom.

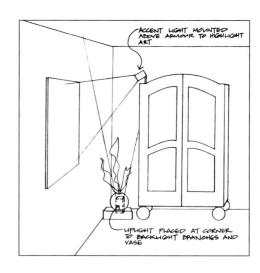

Lighting Designer
Randall Whitehead

Interior Designer
Lilley Yee

Photographer
Russell Abraham

Grace and style are enhanced in this view which looks out from the canopy bed. The soft effect is achieved by the artful placement of an uplight in the far corner which provides backlighting for the branches and vase. Careful highlighting of the specific details renders order to this elegant space.

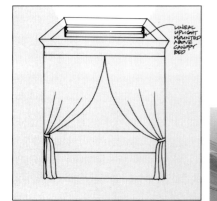

Lighting Designer
Randall Whitehead

Interior Designer
Lilley Yee

Photographer
Russell Abraham

This elegant canopy bed contains a surprise, concealing a subtle up light that sends a soft wash into the ceiling. A suit of armour is both backlit and side lit to reveal its form as a protective presence balancing out another character in this room, an accented statue of Cupid.

Lighting Designer
Michael Souter

Interior Designer
Barbara Jacobs

Photographer
Russell Abraham

A central fixture was replaced with a specially-designed box housing eight recessed downlights. They provide all the accent lighting the room needs.

Lighting Designer
Cynthia Bolton Karasik
and James Benya

Interior Designer
Colleen Roger and Don Simons

Photographer
James Benya

**Backlighted and forelighted
shoji screens add textural
interest to this bedroom.**

Lighting Designer
James Benya

Interior Designer
Sharon Marston

Photographer
James Benya

**Bedside table lamps
provide both task and
gentle fill light for this
luxurious master bedroom.**

Lighting Designer
James Benya

Interior Designer
Sharon Marston

Photographer
James Benya

A shell-shaped rice paper fixture adds visual interest to this reading corner.

Lighting Designer
Cynthia Bolton Karasik
and James Benya

Interior Designer
Gary Hutton

Photographer
James Benya

Wall washers at an acute angle show off the texture of the stone wall.

BATHROOMS
THE GREAT ESCAPE

Well-designed lighting is of the utmost importance in the bathroom, where the activities of grooming and self-care require excellent task lighting. Yet more often than not, homeowners and professionals install fixtures that provide inadequate illumination for tasks at the vanity and other key areas.

Remember when, as a child, you would hold a flashlight under your chin to create a scary face? The same thing happens, only in reverse, when you stand at a vanity directly under a recessed downlight or a single luminaire surface-mounted above the mirror.

Satisfying Vanity at the Vanity

For the most ideal task lighting at a vanity, set up a system of cross-illumination on the vertical axis. This can be accomplished simply by flanking the mirror with two luminaires.

The principle of cross-illumination on the vertical axis originated in the theater, where mirrors were surrounded by bare bulbs. Now homes everywhere have the residential equivalent, multi-bulb brass or chrome light bars. Remember, though, that these bars work best when mounted on either side of the mirror. A third luminaire can be mounted above the mirror, but is not necessary. Light bars aren't your only option: A more recent trend for providing cross-illumination is wall-mounting translucent luminaires at eye level on either side of the sink. Many builders and architects install fluorescent or incandescent light soffits, fitted with either acrylic diffusers or egg-crate louvers, over vanity areas. These fixtures, too, mostly illuminate the top half of a person's face, although some cross-lighting occurs from top to bottom if the light reflects off of a white or glossy counter. While not the optimum solution, this is a passable substitute if vertical cross-illumination is impossible to install.

While the vanity is the most critical spot to illuminate correctly, tubs, showers, and other areas also need good general light. For this purpose, the commonly used

recessed luminaires with white opal diffusers are relatively effective.

Fluorescents in the Bathroom

The fluorescent option is important today. Several states require fluorescent light sources in the design, construction, or remodeling of residential bathrooms, because fluorescents are at least three times more energy efficient than incandescent bulbs.

Fortunately, the color temperature of many of today's fluorescent lamps, including the newer compact fluorescent lamps (CFLs), have color-correcting phosphors that are very flattering to skin tones. Compact fluorescent lamps not only offer greatly improved color rendering, but the 13-watt version, for example, produces illumination similar to that produced by a 60-watt incandescent bulb. Two drawbacks to some of the cheaper compact fluorescent lamps are an inherent hum and the lack of a rapid-start ballast, the latter deficiency causing the lamp to flicker two or three times before stabilizing. Some quad versions are much quieter and have a relatively rapid start-up. These advances, along with long life and dimming capability, make fluorescent lighting worth a second look.

That Special Overall Glow

Indirect lighting in a bathroom adds overall warmth and illumination, even more necessary now that bathrooms are becoming multifunctional spaces. Wall sconces or cove lighting that directs light upward can provide this gentle ambient illumination. Both options can use miniature incandescent lamps, compact fluorescents, or standard-length fluorescent tubes. For bathrooms with higher ceilings, pendant-hung units also can be considered for fill light.

Safety First

The necessity of protecting yourself and your loved ones from electric shock demands special planning when lighting bathrooms. First, make sure that all luminaires located close to water are installed with an instant circuit shutoff, called a ground fault interrupter (GFI). In addition, select only those lighting fixtures that are listed for damp locations by the Underwriters' Laboratory (UL) or another approved testing laboratory. Products tested by the UL have a special blue label.

(Overleaf) Victorian-style wall sconces provide fill lighting for this bathroom, with additional ambient illumination coming from indirect color-corrected fluorescent cove lighting.

Lighting Design and Architecture: Richard Perlstein, AIA
Photo: Muffy Kibbey

All of the light fixtures in this bathroom are fluorescent, now a versatile and energy-efficient alternative to standard incandescent lighting. Of special note, the television is mounted behind the mirror and appears only when turned on.

Lighting Design: Michael Souter,
    IALD, ASID
Interior Design: Bob Miller
Photo: Douglas Salin

In this tight space, sandblasted blown-glass wall

sconces are mounted on the return walls to provide

task lighting at the mirror.

Lighting Design: Randall Whitehead, IALD, ASID
    Affiliate, and Catherine Ng, IES
Interior Design: Helen C. Reuter
Photo: Douglas A. Salin

Compact Murano glass luminaries manufactured by

Zelco were installed flush with the mirror surface,

their housings recessed into the wall before the mirror

installation. The mirror reflects a row of three

additional matching luminaries on the opposite wall.

The fixtures use a 7-watt compact fluorescent lamp.

Lighting Design: Catherine Ng, IES, and
    Randall Whitehead, IALD, ASID Affiliate
Interior Design: Lawrence Masnada
Architecture: Sid Del Mar Leach
Photo: Kenneth Rice

Lighting hidden behind a valence dramatizes the

window treatments, and recessed eyeball fixtures offer

reading light for long, relaxing baths.

Lighting and Interior Design: J. Hettinger Interiors
Photo: Doug Johnson

The design elements of this wild powder room work

together, with the pendant fixture by Christina Spann

reflected in the sheet of glass covering the wall mural.

The pendant provides shadow-free fill light.

Lighting and Interior Design: Lou Ann Bauer
Photo: Douglas A. Salin

Pendant fixtures hover like flying saucers alongside

the two mirrors in this crisply appointed bath.

Daylight floods in through the glass-block wall.

Lighting Design and Architecture: Dan Frederick
Photo: Russell Abraham

A dome detail above the whirlpool sparkles with fiber-

optic stars, while recessed downlights along the

perimeter give off light reminiscent of comets hurtling

toward the heavens.

Lighting Design: Axiom, Inc.
Interior Design: Jim Wallen and Albert Carey
Photo: David Livingston

An indirect linear low-voltage system brings out the

luster of the bathroom's gold-leaf ceiling. Recessed

downlights illuminate the countertops and flooring by

Benattar.

Lighting Design: Axiom, Inc.
Interior Design: Jim Wallen and Albert Carey
Photo: David Livingston

Translucent wall sconces float on the mirrors above the vanity sinks. Fill light comes from the vaulted skylight, which has luminaires mounted within.

Lighting Design: Jared Polsky and Associates
Architecture: Jared Polsky and Associates
Photo: Jay Graham

A blend of natural and artificial light brightens up this master bath. Tall windows provide light during the day, with translucent halogen sconces emitting both task and ambient illumination at night.

Lighting Design: Randall Whitehead, IALD, and
    Catherine Ng, IES
Architecture: Richard Perlstein, AIA
Photo: Muffy Kibbey

Unobtrusive recessed

downlights highlight the

architectural elements and

varied textures.

Lighting/Interior Design and
    Architecture: Charles J.
    Grebmeier, ASID, Grebmeier-
Roy Design
Photo: Eric Zepeda

Pendants in the Arts and Crafts style address the need for task lighting at the vanity (right). The tub is bathed in soft light from fixtures on wall brackets (above). The light well is uplighted to offer additional fill illumination at night.

Lighting Design and Architecture: David Ludwig
Photo: Muffy Kibbey

Lighting Designer
Linda Ferry

Interior Designer
John Schneider

Photographer
Gil Edelstein

Recessed adjustable fixtures add a dramatic flare to this impressive granite bath.

Lighting Designer
Kenton Knapp

Interior Designer
Charles Falls and
Kenton Knapp

Photographer
Eric Zepeda

This sumptuous master bathroom is a sparkly blend of task lighting and ambient illumination. Compact wall bracket fixtures provide the room's fill light, which reduces shadowing on people's faces. The makeup lights surround the mirror to create an even illumination. Recessed lights accent the palm, giving it the appearance of reaching for the skylight above.

Lighting Designer
Catherine Ng and
Randall Whitehead

Interior Designer
Vicky Doubleday and
Peter Gutkin

Photographer
Alan Weintraub

A pendant-hung fixture uses a powerful halogen source suspended below a frosted glass disc to provide the room's fill light. Vertically placed vanity strip fixtures cast a shadowless light for tasks at the sink.

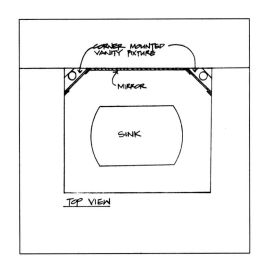

CORNER MOUNTED
VANITY FIXTURE

MIRROR

SINK

TOP VIEW

Lighting Designer
Randall Whitehead

Interior Designer
Sarah Lee Roberts

Photographer
Ben Janken

Incandescent vertically mounted vanity fixtures blend beautifully into the architectural layout of the bathroom.

Lighting Designer
Randall Whitehead
and Catherine Ng

Interior Designer
Gary Hutton

Photographer
Ben Janken

Light fixtures mounted vertically on either side of the sink provide the best illumination for shaving or applying makeup. Here, the fixtures are recessed into the corners so they are flush with the surface of the mirrors. These fixtures use a peach-colored fluorescent bulb that is very compli-mentary to skin tones. The fixtures are dimmable so the intensity of light can be changed without greatly changing the color quality of the light, as is the case with incandescent sources.

Lighting Designer
Randall Whitehead
and Catherine Ng

Interior Designer
Linda Bradshaw-Allen

Photographer
Ben Janken

The wall sconce mounted on the mirror makes this modest bathroom seem much larger.

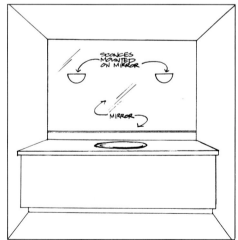

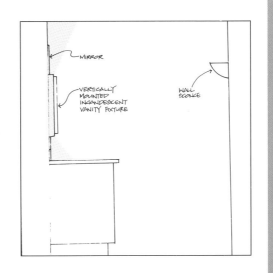

MIRROR

VERTICALLY
MOUNTED
INCANDESCENT
VANITY FIXTURE

WALL
SCONCE

Lighting Designer
Randall Whitehead
and Catherine Ng

Interior Designer
Christian Wright and
Gerald Simpkins

Photographer
Ben Janken

Bathrooms are very task-oriented so it is important to have good cross-illumination at the mirror. Wall sconces (not seen from this angle) generate the overall fill light while a torchiere in the adjoining bedroom throws a pleasant glow of illumination into the space.

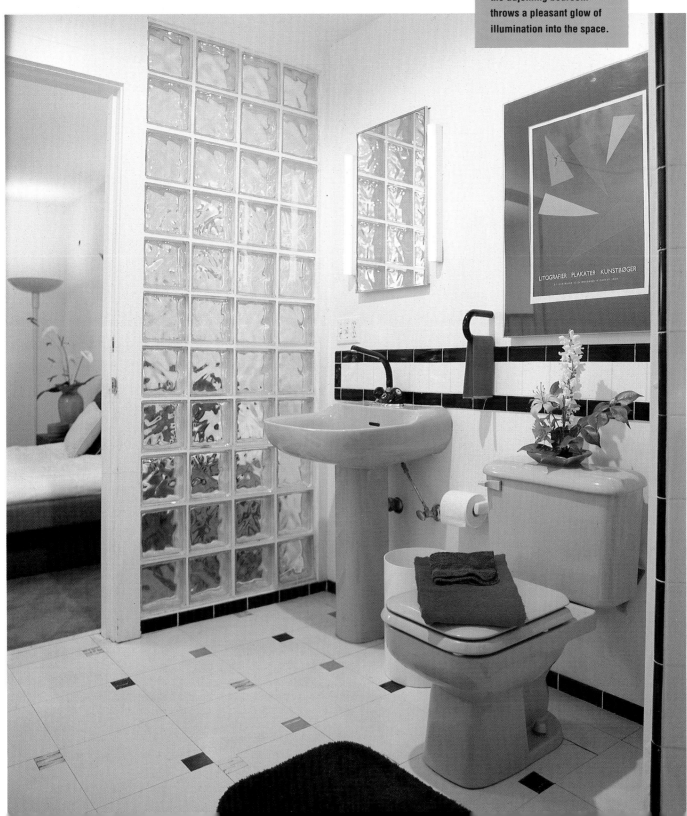

Lighting Designer
Jim Gillam

Interior Designer
Maria Fisher

Photographer
David Livingston

The inventive use of light in this bathroom is enhanced by recessed fixtures spotted onto two glass bowl sinks giving the room an ethereal glow.

Lighting Designer
Linda Ferry

Interior Designer
John Schneider

Photographer
Gil Edelstein

Regressed vertically-mounted vanity lights provide a clean, sophisticated look for this user-friendly bath.

Lighting Designer
Jim Gillam

Interior Designer
Maria Fisher

Photographer
David Livingston

This close-up detail shows the sculptural quality of the glass sinks and how the lighting design effectively enhances it.

Lighting Designer
Kenton Knapp

Interior Designer
Charles Falls and Kenton Knapp

Photographer
Patrick Barta

Individual recessed adjustable fixtures bring these American Indian figures dramatic significance.

Lighting Designer
Sherry Scott

Interior Designer
Sherry Scott

Photographer
Michael L. Krasnobrod

Soft ambient light comes from wall sconces reflecting light off the ceiling in this small but well-designed bathroom.

Lighting Designer
Sherry Scott

Interior Designer
Sherry Scott

Photographer
Michael L. Krasnobrod

This bathroom has space for three people to use the counters simultaneously. The vertical vanity fixtures provide shadowless task light on people's faces for shaving and applying makeup.

COMMERCIAL SPACES

chapter one

Well-designed lighting for a retail store is crucial. A customer's willingness to come in and make a purchase is greatly influenced by their comfort level and their reaction to what they see. A drab, dark, or too-brightly lit store can distract customers from the retailer's main focus—the merchandise.

The entrance of a store should welcome customers and invite them inside. Low-level lighting is a poor choice, since most people have an instinctive aversion to going into dark places: low illumination may make customers feel they are entering a cave. Stores can be overly bright, too. People do not like to be blasted by light, they just want to be invited in. A well-designed lighting plan avoids both extremes by incorporating enough ambient light. Ambient, or fill light, reflecting from walls and ceilings, makes spaces seem larger, and helps all areas of a shop come clearly into view.

Too often, stores put accent light on the merchandise, but neglect overall lighting for the patrons. A lighting design that flatters the customers as much as it does the product works to build sales. Clothing stores in particular have found that if the lighting makes the customers look good, they tend to buy more clothes. Similar to the lighting approach recommended for restaurants, ambient light combined with some task and accent lighting is the most successful plan for retail environments. Unlike restaurant lighting, however, retail lighting must maintain a difficult balance between offering flattering light and light that approximates daylight enough for matching colors.

The projects in this chapter demonstrate innovative approaches to striking this balance while creating lush, exciting spaces.

DR. ALBERT C. LEE
HOURS
MON. - FRI. 11-8
SATURDAY 9-6
SUNDAY 12-5

project   **Urban Eyes Optometry**
             Boutique #1
             San Francisco, CA
lighting   **John Lum Architecture**
architect   **John Lum Architecture**
interior   **John Lum Architecture**
photographer   **Sharon Risedorph**

A flexible, track lighting system mounted above the ceiling line projects a vibrant halogen light to illuminate the structural column. The surface patina is textured with the impressions of the optometric instruments, antique eyewear, and the architect's and optometrist's handprints.

project   **Urban Eyes Optometry**
             Boutique #1
lighting   **John Lum Architecture**
architect   **John Lum Architecture**
interior   **John Lum Architecture**
photographer   **Sharon Risedorph**

Back lighting eyewear is a relatively new concept. Many of today's frames have a translucent quality that shows best when illuminated from behind. Color-corrected fluorescents double as task lights in the storage area located directly behind the Shoji-like display. Simple, dynamic pendant fixtures project light through a hole in the top of these free-standing displays. Single frames get a jewelry store treatment.

Urban Eyes Optometry Boutique San Francisco California

If ever a shop could dispel the myth that glasses are unappealing, it is the Urban Eyes installation on an upscale part of Market Street. The shop's 1,000-square foot interior by John Lum of John Lum Architecture proclaims a decidedly hip and sophisticated atmosphere, sending the subliminal message that customers who sport this eyewear will be equally urbane.

Working closely with lighting designer Randall Whitehead, the architect laid out the space to accommodate product displays and a dispensing area in front, with the more private functions, such as examination room, lab, and offices, in the back. The public front is designed to play with vision and perspective through manipulation of forms, as well as to present a lively exploration of materials and designed objects that will attract passersby into the store.

Inside, one half of the shop is devoted to the display of glasses and the other to dispensing them. For the fun of clients trying on glasses, the atmosphere is similar to that of a modeling runway. Overall lighting comes from recessed fluorescent fixtures, creating the even, glare-free illumination necessary for a retail establishment that is also an optometric health-care practice. Throughout the store, designers kept the light sources as unobtrusive as possible, so that interior elements could be highlighted without extraneous decoration. All of this is accomplished within the tight confines of California's energy-code restrictions.

The sales area is organized along a sinuous wood deck, with eyewear placed between a series of truncated piers—a metaphorical reference to city buildings as well as a practical response to existing columns. Glass shelves between the piers are cleverly illuminated by well lights, eliminating the need for the glare-producing backlit panels typically found in optometric practices. Between each uplight, PL fluorescent fixtures glow behind etched mirrors to create a flattering light. This section is further defined by a wheelchair-accessible wood deck, uplit by well lights.

A perforated metal wall provides additional eyeglass display through the use of removable ribbed plastic shelves. Low-voltage track fixtures mounted on top of the screen highlight the stylized graffiti behind, while recessed MR16 spots add sparkle to the eyeglasses on the adjustable shelves.

Sequestered under the mezzanine stairs is a Buddha shrine and small fish aquarium, elements regarded important to the well being of the store. These niches are illuminated by recessed incandescent "A" lamps, creating a hidden glow that intrigues the customers. The random steel-rod banister expresses a frenetic energy that contrasts with the meditative calmness of the staircase.

project · **Urban Eyes Optometry Boutique #1 San Francisco, CA**
lighting · **John Lum Architecture**
architect · **John Lum Architecture**
interior · **John Lum Architecture**
photographer · **Sharon Risedorph**

Because of the very small square footage of Urban Eyes' first store, the architect employed lighting as a way of making the space seem larger. Creating vignettes within the areas of light and dark visually expands the surroundings. A flexible, miniature track light system highlights the eyewear while producing a cross-hatched shadow effect. These dramatic contrasts produce an intimate atmosphere in keeping with the individualized attention each customer receives in this exclusive boutique.

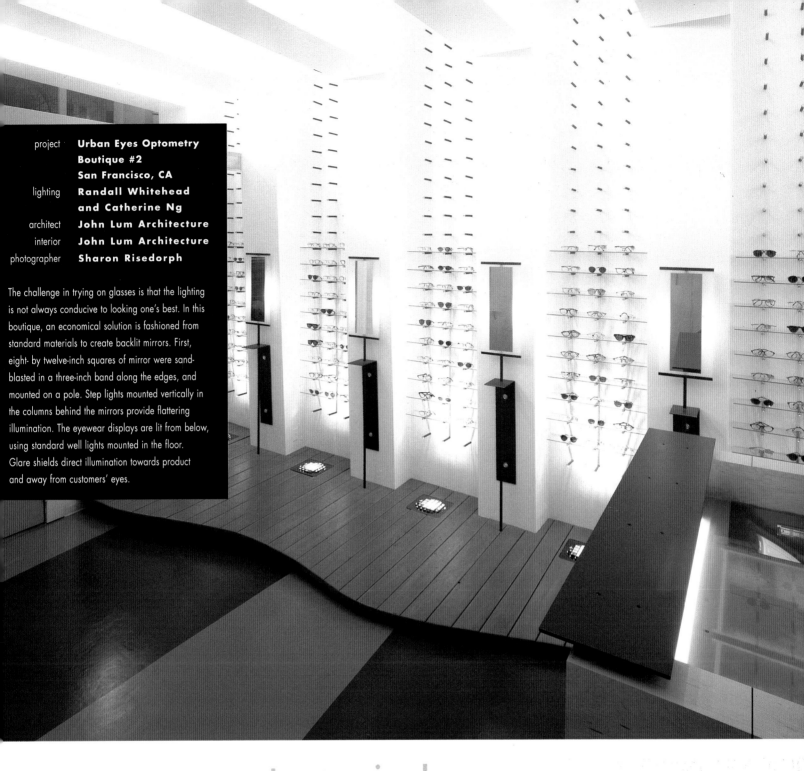

project	**Urban Eyes Optometry Boutique #2 San Francisco, CA**
lighting	**Randall Whitehead and Catherine Ng**
architect	**John Lum Architecture**
interior	**John Lum Architecture**
photographer	**Sharon Risedorph**

The challenge in trying on glasses is that the lighting is not always conducive to looking one's best. In this boutique, an economical solution is fashioned from standard materials to create backlit mirrors. First, eight- by twelve-inch squares of mirror were sandblasted in a three-inch band along the edges, and mounted on a pole. Step lights mounted vertically in the columns behind the mirrors provide flattering illumination. The eyewear displays are lit from below, using standard well lights mounted in the floor. Glare shields direct illumination towards product and away from customers' eyes.

r e t a i l

project	**Urban Eyes Optometry Boutique #1 San Francisco, CA**
lighting	**John Lum Architecture**
architect	**John Lum Architecture**
interior	**John Lum Architecture**
photographer	**Sharon Risedorph**

A close-up view of shadow play and progressive eyewear treatment.

project	**Confetti Chocolat**
	San Francisco, CA
lighting	**Alan and Joy Ohashi**
architect	**Ohashi Design Studio**
interior	**Ohashi Design Studio**
photographer	**Russell Abraham**

Confetti Chocolat is a highly successful retail store combining gourmet coffee and candy sales in a festive environment with an Italian flavor. This was achieved by separating coffee sales (at left) from chocolate candy sales (center), and carefully studying the layout of coffee equipment so that the queuing up for morning or lunch time coffee did not interfere with the more leisurely browsing for candy. The lighting was designed to be high key, focusing spots, floods, and wall washers on only the merchandise or serving counters to create highlights and shadows for a lively retail environment.

project
The Peppercorn
Carmel, CA

lighting
Donald Maxcy

interior
Donald Maxcy

photographer
Ron Starr

At night, lighting identifies the store's merchandise and continues to "sell" after closing hours—taking advantage of foot traffic past the storefront in the early evening.

project
**Kimono Shop
Tokyo, Japan**
lighting
TL Yamagiwa Lab.
interior
Masanori Umeda
photographer
Yoshio Shiratori

[top] The careful composition of panels in the shapes of clouds, lightning, and rain create an evocative, glowing backdrop.

[bottom] The shapes of clouds, the moon, and migratory birds have been clipped out from an aluminum sheet, like a Kabuki set, (one of the traditional entertainments of Japan). Adjustable backlighting gives the impression of light reflecting off water, shimmering through the openwork. Products displayed on staggered shelves appear to float.

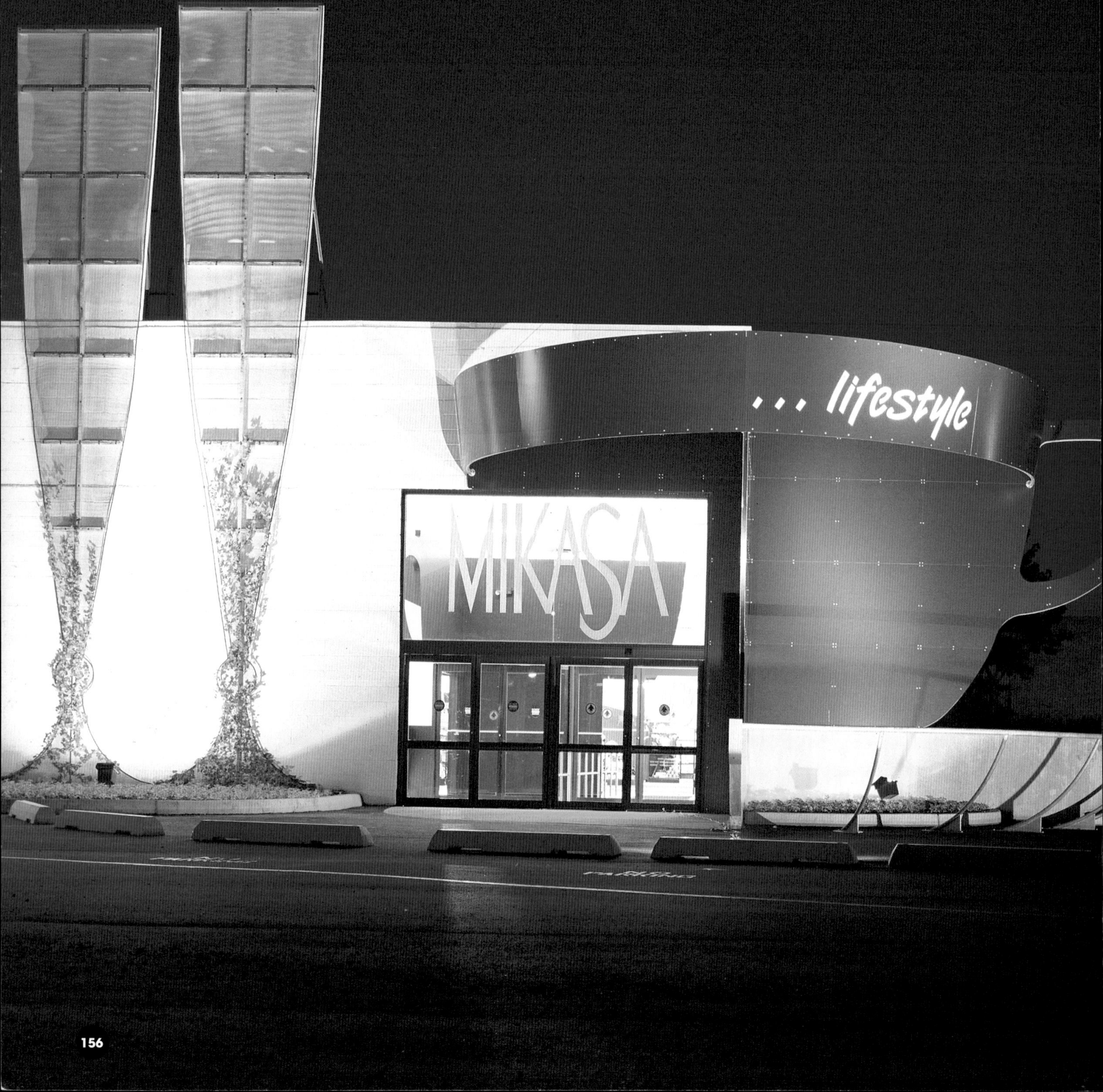
... lifestyle
MIKASA

project
**Mikasa...lifestyle
Secaucus, NJ**
lighting
Paul Haigh
architect
**Haigh Architects
Designers**
interior
**Paul Haigh and
Barbara Haigh**
photographer
Elliot Kaufman

The main entrance is floodlit with exterior-rated halogen fixtures. The entrance vestibule is lit with green-hued fluorescent, while the exit vestibule is lit with red-hued fluorescent.

project   **Mikasa...lifestyle
            Secaucus, NJ**
lighting   **Paul Haigh**
architect   **Haigh Architects Designers**
interior   **Paul Haigh and Barbara Haigh**
photographer **Elliot Kaufman**

The view of the interior shows the displays and check-out area. An ambient system of industrial fluorescent fixtures positioned to reflect from the underside of the roof deck is balanced by a grid of Par 38 spots on extension wands, aimed to highlight the displayed merchandise.

project
CompUSA
New York, NY
lighting
William Whistler, Brennan Beer
Gorman Monk / Interiors
architect
Sharad Gokarna, Brennan Beer
Gorman Monk / Interiors
interior
William Whistler, Brennan Beer
Gorman Monk / Interiors
photographer
Peter Paige

The curved display wall is lighted with pendant-mounted circular lights, hung flush with the under side of the ceiling grid and painted to match the dark gray structure.

project	**CompUSA**
	New York, NY
lighting	**William Whistler,**
	Brennan Beer Gorman Monk / Interiors
architect	**Sharad Gokarna,**
	Brennan Beer Gorman Monk / Interiors
interior	**William Whistler,**
	Brennan Beer Gorman Monk / Interiors
photographer	**Peter Paige**

The painted sheetrock facia and soffit provide a finished architectural presentation to pedestrians at the retail level, and are complementary to the office tower architecture above. The pale gray reflects light softly, yet creates definition in the retail space.

retail

project
**Smith and Hawken
Stores
Berkeley, CA**

lighting
**Larry French,
S. Leonard Auerbach
& Associates**

architect
Forrest Architects

interior
Forrest Architects

photographer
Douglas A. Salin

The challenge for Smith and Hawken, a gardening and accessories store, was to balance natural light and artificial light in a dynamic way. The warehouse feel of the space was accentuated with surface conduit wiring. Yellow wall-mounted fixtures provide a flexible, easily accessible accent light for displays.

project **Smith and Hawken Stores
Berkeley, CA**
lighting **Larry French, S. Leonard
Auerbach & Associates**
architect **Forrest Architects**
interior **Forrest Architects**
photographer **Douglas A. Salin**

A series of well proportioned pendants, using metal halide lamps, produces a comfortable fill light in a color temperature complementary to the natural light coming in through store windows and skylights. The special ribbed glass adds some sparkle without causing glare.

project   **Broadway Market**
           Seattle, WA
lighting   **Christopher**
           Thompson
architect **Cardwell / Thomas**
           & Associates Inc.
photographer **David Story**

An intimate shopping atmosphere is created
by diffuse illumination from the skylights, along
with the warm, colorful lighting of the booths
and shops.

retail

project
**Broadway Market
Seattle, WA**

lighting
**Christopher
Thompson**

architect
**Cardwell / Thomas
& Associates Inc.**

photographer
David Story

The curved display wall is
lighted with pendant mounted
circular lights, hung flush with
the under side of the ceiling
grid and painted to match the
dark gray structure.

RESTAURANTS

eating well and looking fabulous

c h a p t e r   t w o

A whole new breed of restaurant designers have redefined what it means to go out to dinner. Choices are no longer limited to seats under a hot spotlight, or candlelit alcoves so dark that diners have to fumble for the first course. A wonderful sense of theater has been thrown into the mix, and the result is restaurants that don't sacrifice good lighting for good looks.

Lighting design plays a major role in defining the atmosphere of a restaurant's interior and exterior. Inside, it flatters both the restaurant's design *and* its diners; outside it advertises the restaurant by night with fixtures that don't obscure the building by day.

Ambient light is now getting top billing in most restaurant designs, often coupled with accent lighting to highlight art and greenery.

Designs where each table is illuminated by a spotlight, making diners appear ghoulish the moment they sit down and lean forward, are giving way to those incorporating gentle uplighting from pendant lights, cove lighting, and even votive candles.

The light of track and spot lighting is harsh on faces, it illuminates only the nose, making people's eye sockets seem to recede into blackness.

The effect is similar to holding a flashlight under your chin. The softer effect of ambient lighting takes some planning, especially in restaurants with dark-colored ceilings that don't reflect light well, but is well worth the investment. The ambient effects in the projects that follow demonstrate techniques used by top restaurant designers to flatter both the customers and the cuisine.

project	**Cypress Club**
	San Francisco, CA
lighting	**Jordan Mozer**
architect	**Jordan Mozer**
interior	**Jordan Mozer**
photographer	**Dennis Anderson**

In the Cypress Club dining room, big, round, polka-dotted chandeliers and pillow-like sculptural copper structures separate levels of the dining room, casting a warm amber-toned light similar to the color of beer in a glass.

project	**Cypress Club**
	San Francisco, CA
lighting	**Jordan Mozer**
architect	**Jordan Mozer**
interior	**Jordan Mozer**
photographer	**Dennis Anderson**

project
Cypress Club
San Francisco, CA
lighting
Jordan Mozer
architect
Jordan Mozer
interior
Jordan Mozer
photographer
Dennis Anderson

Sculptural copper "pillows" separate the dining room's two levels. The shape of the dining room chairs were inspired by the fenders of a 1948 "Hudson" car. Lighting is soft and amber in tone, in harmony with the curvy surroundings. The chicken-like sconces on the walls are made of cast bronze and slumped glass, and shaped appropriately for a restaurant resembling a chicken in a prep kitchen more than a one crossing the street.

Cypress Club San Francisco California

Jordan Mozer found his inspiration for the Cypress Club in Hollywood's version of San Francisco during the forties. The club's name derives from a fictional restaurant in Raymond Chandler's novel *The Big Sleep*. The design features squat, bigger-than-life columns, ballooning light fixtures, and overstuffed furniture, resulting in a space where Mozer feels "you might find Clark Kent or Roger Rabbit." Curvy forms from 1940s industrial design, such as the 1948 Hudson car, airplanes, vacuum cleaners, and television sets, decorate the interior, illuminated by the type of soft, indirect lighting favored by fashion photographers.

The entire club is a wild, wonderful indoor fantasy that conjures up images from the whole spectrum of one's imagination; another world down to the last detail, including dishes, furniture, and light fixtures. Maple, mahogany, copper, marble, and stained glass are all part of the look. Diners feel instantly comfortable, with a slight sense of having been there before.

The lighting design creates a warm, flattering light for romantic dining. Indirect light is the main source of illumination, to avoid any intrusive glare. Lots of uplighting reflects from diffusing materials, including the rich cream, ruby, and amber tones of blown and slumped glass fixtures.

At the center of the room, luminaires have sprinkler heads dropped through their centers. They are positioned to bounce light from the cream-colored velvet drapes that hang above them (covering electrical drops and speakers in the ceiling.) Fondly referred to as the "Parachuting Donut" lamps, these fixtures are made of blown glass and spun aluminum, as are related fixtures throughout the room.

The perimeter mural is painted in the Depression-era, Work Program style, and is a visual tour of northern California. Elegantly integrated, the Cypress Club's lighting and design elements come together to create a soft, fluid, and lyrical space.

project	**Cypress Club**
	San Francisco, CA
lighting	**Jordan Mozer**
architect	**Jordan Mozer**
interior	**Jordan Mozer**
photographer	**Dennis Anderson**

Pin spotlights provide accent lighting for tabletops, artwork, and displays.

r e s t a u r a n t s

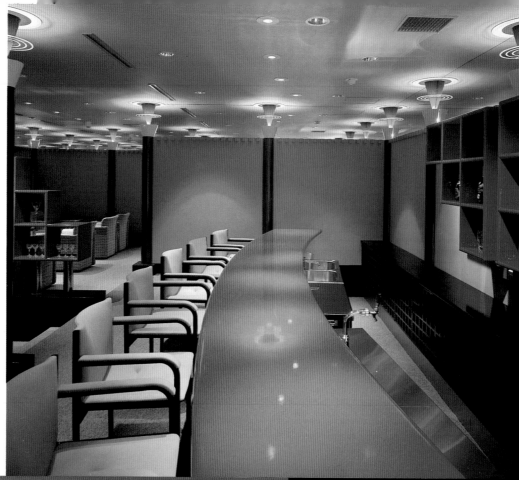

project
**Beer Restaurant,
Aoyama City
Tokyo, Japan**
lighting
TL Yamagiwa Lab
interior
Masanori Umeda
photographer
Yoshio Shiratori

A shiny red counter slices the space like a Japanese sword. Whimsical "outer space" ceiling-mounted fixtures provide subtle downlighting.

project   **Silks Restaurant,
Mandarin Oriental Hotel
San Francisco, CA**
lighting   **Randall Whitehead and
Catherine Ng**
interior   **James Marzo Design**
photographer   **John Vaughan**

Recessed accent luminaires bring out the colors of the painting. The custom fixtures become part of the atmosphere, instead of overpowering or simply fading into the background.

project   **Zenith Restaurant
Denver, CO**
lighting   **Clanton Engineering**
interior   **Gensler and Associates**
photographer   **Marco Lorenzetti**

The main dining areas feature a gray carpet, white table linens, and black chairs. The walls are white polymix. Cove lighting in the ceiling shines down into the dining space through perforated metal panels. A cylinder penetrating a black disk forms a table that holds a dramatic display of flowers and desserts. Additional lighting in the dining area is from low-voltage lights on a cable system. The walls are a white polymix.

project	**Regina Chi Chi Beignet**
	San Francisco, CA
lighting	**Randall Whitehead,**
	Catherine Ng
architect	**Huntsman Associates**
interior	**Jessica Hall**
photographer	**Dennis Anderson**

Playful "cuckoo's nest" pendant fixtures by Christina Spann invite
diners into the party-like atmosphere of this space. A framing
projector creates a star pattern at the far end of the restaurant,
the visual reward for making the long trip from the front door.

project **Longshoreman's Daughter Seattle, WA**
lighting **Brendt Markee**
architect **Rik Adams**
interior **Adams / Mohler Architects**
photographer **Robert Pisano**

In this overall view of the restaurant, Calder-like pendants soar above the tables. Light-colored disks act as reflectors to produce good ambient light.

project **Spot Bagel Bakery Wallingford Seattle, WA**
lighting **Adams / Mohler Architects**
architect **Rik Adams and Rick Mohler**
interior **Adams / Mohler Architects**
photographer **Steve Keating**

In the condiment area, pendants float above the tables and giant lava-lamp-topped sconces punctuate the bench.

project	**Spot Bagel Bakery**
	Newmark
	Seattle, WA
lighting	**Adams / Mohler Architects**
architect	**Rik Adams and Rick Mohler**
interior	**Adams / Mohler Architects**
photographer	**Robert Pisano**

This view of the seating area and spiral, sheet-metal column demonstrates how circline fluorescents help this "spaceship" lift off. Custom pendants of perforated metal and glowing rings are suspended over the bar, while huge, lava-lamp-topped luminaires hover over the tables.

project	**Sushi Kinta Restaurant San Francisco, CA**
lighting	**Alan and Joy Ohashi**
architect	**Alan and Joy Ohashi**
interior	**Alan and Joy Ohashi**
photographer	**John Sutton**

Located near a busy pedestrian thoroughfare, a twelve-foot long, neon-lit fish sign attracts passersby. Bronze-colored mirrors and focused, high-key, low-voltage, cable-mounted lighting enhance the surroundings without distracting diners. The use of white plastic laminate and maple cabinets creates a sense of cleanliness, order, and simplicity.

project	**Cafe 817 Oakland, CA**
lighting	**Randall Whitehead**
architect	**Teresa Sevilla**
interior	**Robert Josten**
photographer	**J.D. Peterson**

A seismic frame at the back of this narrow space posed an aesthetic hurdle. A hole that echoes the shape of the frame was made in the back wall, and covered with metal mesh. Fixtures mounted to the sides illuminate the screen as a translucent element. A cable system does the accent lighting while pendants designed by Pam Morris add the glowing fill lights.

project	**Azur Restaurant and Ballroom**
	Minneapolis, MN
lighting	**Michael DiBlasi**
architect	**Gregory Rothweiler**
interior	**Richard D'Amico, D'Amico and Partners, Inc.,**
	Gregory Rothweister, Shea Architects
photographer	**Christian Korab**

Theatrical pattern projectors and theatrical fixtures with colored gels light the fabric-draped ceiling. Custom, double, glue-chipped and back-painted pendants are suspended between

project   **Aqua Restaurant**
           San Francisco, CA
lighting   **Larry French**
architect   **Frost and Tsuchi**
interior   **Frost and Tsuchi**
photographer **Douglas A. Salin**

Architectural details flanking the huge mirrors
throughout the space are subtly fore- and backlighted to show off the textural quality of the
wall surfaces. Individual votive candles produce
pleasing islands of illumination at each table.
The entry makes a subtle statement. The feeling
is calming to the eye and sets up the anticipation of a sumptuous meal.

project   **The Backstage Restaurant**
            San Francisco, CA
lighting   **Terry Ohm**
photographer **Charles Cormany**

Small Lightolier monopoints are used to highlight the ivory-colored columns surrounding the room. The steel sconces, formed in the shapes of ivy branches, emit a soft indirect light from behind each leaf. The balance of the lighting is achieved with custom-designed floor lamps and wall sconces to create the intimate atmosphere of a living room.

project   **P.F. Changs**
             China Bistro
             Scottsdale, AZ
lighting   **Pam Ackerman**
architect   **Rick Schreiber**
interior   **Ann McKenzie**
photographer **Mark Boisclair**
             Photography, Inc.

Custom designed, floating, circular metal and canvas discs are suspended mysteriously over the dining floor. Low-voltage cable lights dash across space from statues to walls. Track lights float overhead like stars in the dark sky.

HOTELS

sumptuous satisfaction for guests

chapter three

Hotels can represent the ultimate lighting challenge. The objective is two-fold: first, to make guests feel at home, so they can relax and be comfortable, second, to create areas of dramatic visual interest—so that people will be attracted to and impressed with the surroundings. Lighting sets the tone for the whole environment: from the building entryway to the guest suites and bathrooms, it is the critical element in creating a first-class hotel atmosphere.

Lighting of outside areas, building facades, and signage must be carefully designed to help lead patrons into the building. Too often, one drives into a large hotel complex, or walks down a street toward one, and it is not readily apparent where to enter the building or how to get to the registration desk. This design flaw is easily corrected through proper lighting. A subtle splash of light around the entrance will naturally draw people's attention. Highlighting the reception area will attract traffic in that direction.

These techniques don't have to be flashy, they can remain unobtrusive and well-integrated into the overall design.

Hotel suites themselves should have lighting that is similar to residential lighting, with comfort and convenience the key factors in the design. Ambient light, reflected from walls and ceilings, should be the main light source in the room. Wall sconces and torchieres are a good way to achieve this effect. Table lamps can be used, but

should have opaque shades to eliminate glare. Indirect lighting will give rooms soft, comfortable, but adequate illumination, which will allow people to work or relax without distraction.

Bath lighting is also very important. The way a guest feels is strongly affected by how they see themselves in the mirror. For task light at the vanity, use fixtures flanking the mirror, to evenly illuminate the entire face. Fixtures mounted above the

mirror cast unflattering shadows, making people look tired and older than they really are. The rule of thumb, especially for hotels, is to always put people in their best light.

Because hotel projects require a tiered lighting approach, successful hotel lighting is really at the cutting edge; demonstrating how remarkably far the hospitality industry and its designers will go to create the perfect retreat.

project   **St. Regis Hotel, New York, NY**

lighting   **Gustin Tan, Brennan Beer Gorman Monk / Interiors**
               Theo Kondos, T. Kondos Associates

architect   **Julia F. Monk, Brennan Beer Gorman Monk / Interiors**

interior   **David W. Beer, Brennan Beer Gorman Monk / Interiors**

photographer   **Anthony P. Albarello**

In lighting the exterior of the original building, the design team sought to highlight the windows and carved Indiana limestone. On the small balconies flanking the sides of the old building, 35-watt high-pressure sodium lamps provide uplighting. At the third level, 400-watt lamps highlight the three-level architectural element where the next molding occurs. Two hundred and fifty-watt lamps light the roof from the 15th and 16th floors.

project
**The Governor Hotel
Portland, OR**
lighting
Candra Scott
architect
Candra Scott
interior architect
**Candra Scott and
The Malder Company**
interior
Candra Scott
photographer
Langdon Clay

[previous page]
The lobby area features a larger-than-life size mural of Lewis and Clark's journey from Celilo Falls down the Columbia to Fort Clatsop, and Sacajawea overlooking the ocean as she saw it for the first time. Custom designed furniture with hand-painted feather and diamond motifs, taken from the original architectural details, continues this theme in the 100 guest rooms. Leaf patterns decorate both the column-based standing lamps and massive, hanging fixtures.

project	**The Manhattan**
	Chiba, Japan
lighting	**Paul Marantz,**
	Kaoru Mende
interior architect	**Candra Scott**
interior	**Candra Scott**
photographer	**Yoshiteru Baba**

The interior decoration of the hospitality suites differs from suite to suite, each named after a celebrity and capturing a moment from a classic movie. The Humphrey Bogart suite is in a tailored 1940s style, paneled in deep rich tones of mahogany. Period sconces give the room an intimate atmosphere, while recessed spotlights and sculptural pendants provide abundant task light for conferences.

The Manhattan Tokyo Japan

The design inspiration for this 130-room luxury hotel evolved both from the hotel's name, The Manhattan, and from its architectural design, which recalls the silhouette of the Chrysler Building in New York City.

The design team, headed by Candra Scott, decided to recreate the glamour of New York City from the mid-1920s until 1940. Many months of research on the Art Deco period were necessary to produce authentically-designed interiors, as well as to locate original Art Deco furniture and lighting fixtures for the project.

The lobby combines period lighting and furniture with luxurious, custom-designed pieces from the 1925 Paris Exhibition. Light falling on the rich palette of soft greens, golds, and reds creates a feeling of warmth and comfort.

The hotel's restaurant was inspired by the famous Parisian brasserie La Coupole. The room's many columns are illuminated with a soft wash of light from lamps hidden in the molding below. Recessed can lights in the ceiling wash three large murals depicting *The Grand Voyage*. The original chandeliers are vintage from the Ziegfeld. Designed to mimic the style of an elegant New York mansion, the room's rich wood tones and luxuriously upholstered golden walls reflect light warmly and create a beautiful setting for any occasion.

Accurate period style follows through into every space of the hotel. The Parlor is influenced by small smoking rooms found in hotels and theaters of the period. Ceiling lights are recessed in a soffit to accent the copper leaf ceiling. Can lights wash light over murals and the Parlor's cork-banded walls. Thirties-vintage floor lamps of chrome and green glass offer task lighting, without marring the carefully created fantasy.

The interior decoration of the hospitality suites, like the rest of the hotel, hides functionality behind luxury. The Humphrey Bogart suite has a tailored, 1940s style, with recessed can lights in a coffered ceiling, and paneling in deep, rich tones of mahogany. The Greta Garbo quarters contains floor lamps with black and gold painted bases and alabaster bowl tops. Stunning jewel tones throughout the room portray the opulence of Paris in the 1930s. The Bette Davis suite honors the ultimate grande dame with the richness and warmth of a traditional mansion, including matching chandeliers and sconces, and floor lamps with carved, gold leaf bases.

Since the rooms on this floor are very popular for small receptions and business meetings, it was especially important that they have an intimate, residential atmosphere. The lighting is designed to create an overall, ambient glow, while providing task light above the conference and dining tables.

project	**The Manhattan Chiba, Japan**
lighting	**Paul Marantz, Kaoru Mende**
interior architect	**Candra Scott**
interior	**Candra Scott**
photographer	**Yoshiteru Baba**

The lobby combines original Art Deco lighting and furniture, as well as luxurious custom designed pieces from the 1925 Paris exhibition. The rich palette of soft greens, golds, and reds creates a feeling of warmth and comfort. Recessed spot lighting strengthens the illusion that light is streaming from the painting on the wall. Dramatic uplighting enhances architectural features.

h o t e l s

project **The Governor Hotel Portland, OR**
lighting **Candra Scott**
architect **Candra Scott**
interior **Candra Scott and The Malder Company**
interior **Candra Scott**
photographer **Langdon Clay**

The artwork for the guestrooms was inspired by Lewis and Clark's journal illustrating nature, flora, and fauna. Each guest room door is appointed with an Indian wall sconce, which throws a romantic "torch" light. Painted feather and diamond motifs, taken from the original architectural details, continues this theme in the 100 guest rooms. leaf patterns decorate both the column-based standing lamps and massive, hanging fixtures.

project **Palace of the Lost City Sun City, South Africa**
lighting **Ross De Alessi**
architect **Wimberly Allison Tong & Goo**
interior **Wilson & Associates**
photographer **Courtesy of Sun International**

In the porte-cochère entry to The Palace of the Lost City sculpture and architectural features are lit from beneath to create a fantastic, theatrical effect.

project **Palace of the Lost City Sun City, South Africa**
lighting **Ross De Alessi**
architect **Wimberly Allison Tong & Goo**
interior **Wilson & Associates**
photographer **Courtesy of Sun International**

In the "Elephant Court" doorway and balcony lighting evokes a torch lit Eastern Palace.

project
**Plaza Las Fuentes
Hotel
Pasadena, CA**
architect
Moore Rubell Yudell
interior
Babey–Moulton, Inc.
photographer
Jaime Ardiles Arce

Massive hanging chandeliers dominate the aesthetics of this passage, providing the general illumination and an intriguing design element. Seating groups are each in the warm light of a large table lamp. Lit upper balconies create definition and add perspective to the space.

179

project **Hyatt Regency**
San Francisco, CA
lighting *principal designers*
Patricia Glasow and Len Auerbach
lighting designer
Virva Kokkonen
architect **ELS / Elbasoni & Logan Architects**
interior **Hirsch / Bedner Associates**
photographer **John Sutton Photography**

[above] The Cafe uses a low-voltage open conductor wire system spanning up to 60 feet. Twenty-watt narrow spot MR16 lamps illuminate tables, plants, and artwork, as well as the stepped ceiling above the atrium floor.

[right] Grazing light accents walls, foliage, and elevator shafts in the atrium. PAR64 spotlights define pedestrian paths and sculpture.

project	**The Triton Hotel**
	San Francisco, CA
lighting	**Terry Ohm**
architect	**Wil Wong**
interior	**Michael Moore**
photographer	**John Vaughan**

The torchiere, fabricated from brushed steel, offers a contrast of whimsical lines with an industrial edge, creating an environment that offers both comfort and visual stimulation to the Triton's visitors.

project   **Holiday Inn Express**
          Osaka Utsubo Park
          Osaka, Japan
lighting   **·Yukio Oka**
architect   **Kazuhiro Motomochi**
interior   **Kazuhiro Motomochi**
photographer   **Atelier Fukumoto**

[left]   Pass-through lighting is provided by the incandescent downlights. The designer created these unique sandblasted torchieres, which illuminate the fresco painting on the ceiling and also help create diffuse, inviting light for the space.

[below]   Punch lighting is provided through a series of incandescent downlights. Attractive indirect lighting comes from the cove and the soffit. The designer created the unusual olive leaf-shaped fixtures for the walls and ceiling. The fixtures help to convey the hotel's theme, which is based on ancient Greek myths.

project   **Dai Ichi Hotel Tokyo,**
          Tokyo, Japan
lighting   **Naomi Miller, Bradley A. Bouch,**
          Takae Oyake, Luminae Souter
          Lighting Design
architect   **Mitsubishi Estate Co., Ltd.**
interior   **Media Five Limited**
photograher   **Courtesy of Lutron**

Neon and fiber-optic lighting allow for special effects ranging from a simulated star field to a midnight-blue sky effect. Fluorescent wall-slot fixtures highlight the simulated outdoor trompe l'oeil wall. Recessed incandescent fixtures provide the ambient light, and decorative pendants, wall sconces and table lamps provide ambient light, style, and elegance to the interiors.

project	**Palace Ai Yahata**
	Fukuoka, Japan
lighting	**Kenji Kitani, Kousaku Matsumoto**
architect	**Seiji Tanaka, Ikuei Ikeda**
interior	**Seiji Tanaka, Hiroshi Kawaguchi**
photographer	**Masaaki Fukumoto**

The entrance is designed to create a South Seas island feeling. During the day it is bright, with natural light and glass that evokes the blue colors of the sea. At night, it has a very different look, as a "starry sky" emerges.

project
Grand Hyatt Bali
Bali, Indonesia
lighting
Jeff Miller
architect
Sydney C.L. Char,
Wimberly Allison Tong & Goo;
Naokazu Hanadoh
and Kazubiko Kuroka,
Shimizu Corp.
interior
Hirsh Bedner & Associates
photographer
Donna Day

The architects wanted a design that fit
unobtrusively into the fragile environment of
the island of Bali, and were inspired by the
Balinese village. Buildings with courtyards were
decentralized for an intimate setting. In this
dawn view through the entry colonades,
luminaires atop the columns provide a soft fill
light, in keeping with the intimate atmosphere.
The reception building is designed to resemble
a Balinese water palace.

project **Granlibakken Resort**
Tahoe City, CA
lighting **Randall Whitehead**
architect **Jeffrey A. Lundahl**
Todd B. Lankenau
interior **Sylvia Stevens**
photographer **Donna Kempner**

A plain T-bar grid ceiling with two- by four-foot
fluorescent lights was proposed for this conference
center. An imaginative redesign by the project
architect produced this stepped coffer detail using
dimmable color-corrected fluorescent lamps.
The three dimensional theme is picked up by semi-
circular sconces "floating" on mirrors, creating an
illusion of depth and space.

project **Resort at Squaw Creek**
Squaw Creek, CA
lighting **Bradley A. Bouch,**
Jim Benya,
Luminae Souter
Lighting Design
architect **Ward Young Architects**
interior **Simon Martin – Vegue**
Winkelstein Moris
photographer **Chas McGrath**

Entering the lobby, the indoor space echoes nature's
colors on a warmer, more human scale. The designers
underscored the inherent opulence of the natural
materials, which include flame granite in the floors,
granite boulders taken from the site, and rough-hewn
Douglas fir framed chairs. Recessed spotlights create
sculptural shadows on the massive stone columns,
while hanging fixtures create pools of light to lead
patrons toward the information desk.

project
**Hyatt Regency
San Francisco
International Airport
Burlingame, CA**
lighting
**Mark Hornberger,
Hornberger & Worstell and
Vladimir Bazjanac, Ph.D.**
architect
Jack J. Worstell
interior
Architectural Interiors
photographer
Sally Painter

[left] A translucent, teflon-coated fiberglass fabric roof stretches across the 39,000 square foot atrium space. Natural light filters through the translucent fabric, providing ideal daylighting conditions for tree growth, and diffuse, ambient lighting for hotel functions.

[below] Subtly lit columns make this an intimate setting within the atrium. Accent lights mounted on the overlapping grid highlight the tables and plants.

HOUSES OF WORSHIP
h e a v e n   o n   e a r t h

c h a p t e r   f o u r

It is distressing to walk into a beautiful church, temple, or cathedral and find an inspiring interior that no one can appreciate because the lighting is so poorly done! Spiritual sanctuaries seem to suffer the most from incorrect illumination, because their sensitive designs can easily be lost amid glaring lights, or dark corners and ceilings. Stained-glass windows are almost always neglected, which is especially unfortunate since the possibilities are

endless for increasing their visual presence through the use of lighting.

A soft glow of ambient illumination is particularly important in a spiritual gathering place, where the atmosphere can easily be shattered by invasive downlights or spotlights. Gentle fill light can, at the same time, serve to illuminate ceilings and walls, and to bring out delicate detailing and woodwork carvings. It also can be bright enough to

provide illumination for parishioners to read songs, prayers, or scripture. Too often, harsh downlights are used for this purpose; a poor choice, since downlights tend to glare and can actually make reading more difficult. Downlights also cast unflattering shadows on people's faces.

As lighting designers we lament, *why go to the trouble of creating sublimely beautiful atmospheric effects if they are lit too poorly for people*

to see? Even the most humble church setting benefits from artful lighting, to enhance the visitor's experience of worship.

Theatrical lighting techniques are useful for lighting a house of worship, where lighting serves many of the same functions as in a theater: there must be adequate ambient light for the audience, the key players must be highlighted, and the set must be carefully illuminated, so that it is apparent without overshadowing the people.

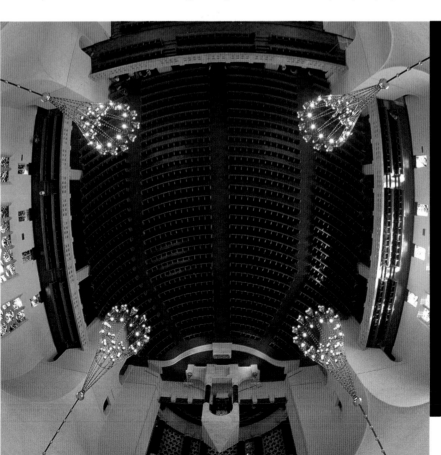

project
**Temple Emanu El Sanctuary
San Francisco, CA**
lighting
**Len Auerbach
Larry French**
architect
David Robinson
photographer
Bob Swanson

[left] Although the chandeliers deliver a considerable amount of general light into the room, the quality is so even that the surfaces tended to flatten. In particular, the dome interior was so generally lit that the sense of a curved surface receding from the viewer was lost. Along with complete cleaning, rewiring, and relamping, custom uplight fixtures were added around the interior perimeter of the lower band of each chandelier.

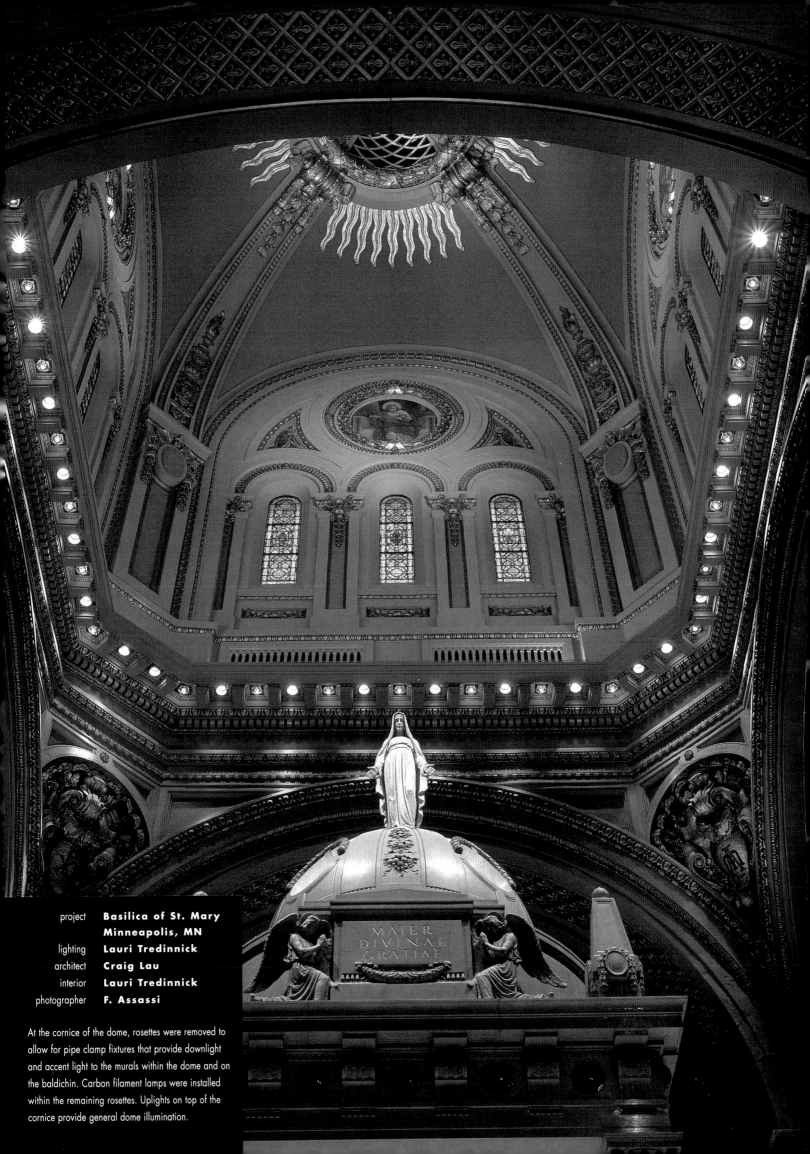

project	**Basilica of St. Mary**
	Minneapolis, MN
lighting	**Lauri Tredinnick**
architect	**Craig Lau**
interior	**Lauri Tredinnick**
photographer	**F. Assassi**

At the cornice of the dome, rosettes were removed to allow for pipe clamp fixtures that provide downlight and accent light to the murals within the dome and on the baldichin. Carbon filament lamps were installed within the remaining rosettes. Uplights on top of the cornice provide general dome illumination.

project **St. Stephen's Church Belvedere, CA**
lighting **Randall Whitehead**
architect **Harold Hansen**
photographer **Ben Janken**

[above] Thanks to a new lighting design plan, the stained glass windows of the church can be seen at night.

[below] This schematic drawing, shown to the parishioners, depicts how the new wall sconces would be mounted to the columns. The top view shows the compact metal halide source, located in the upper half of the luminaire.

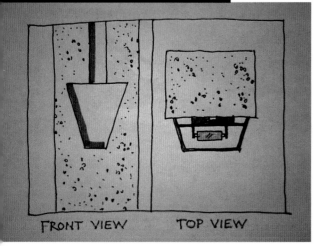

FRONT VIEW   TOP VIEW

St. Stephen's Church Belvedere California

St. Stephen's Church has a ceiling with a 40-foot peak. When its parishioners painted the aging concrete vault an azure blue that no one could see from the ground, they realized it would take more than paint to lighten up the atmosphere.

The cast concrete church structure was built in 1953. Its original wiring ran through the walls in conduits that accommodated a maximum of five circuits for the lighting of the 80-foot by 30-foot ceiling space. The original lighting—rows of 300-watt PAR 38 lamps in porcelain sockets running in a wooden trough between the columns—pointed down from 20 feet, leaving the ceiling in darkness.

When the congregation decided to bring light to the newly painted ceiling, they called in lighting designer Randall Whitehead. His challenge was to solve the lighting problem within the power limitations imposed by the structure, and to find a way to hide any new wiring in a poured concrete building. The designer created a system that allows members to light the church in a variety of ways for different times and purposes.

The existing trough is fitted with a new bottom and recessed adjustable fixtures, using 90-watt PAR quartz lamps directed toward the walls. The design extends wiring from the troughs down the columns, hiding it in the routed back of a trim board stained gray to match the concrete. Halfway down each column, about ten feet from the floor, the designer installed custom luminaires that provide uplighting and downlighting at the same time. Uplighting comes from 250-watt, 4100 Kelvin metal halide sources, and downlighting from 150-watt R40 blue filtered incandescent "jeweler's lamps" with a color temperature close to that of the metal halide.

The three adjustable, 45-watt quartz PAR 38 lamps are mounted on the wall near the floor to accent the Christ figure. The incandescents,

whether dimmed to a reddish hue, or turned up to a more golden glow, offer a pointed contrast to the rest of the lighting. Trough fixtures, accent lights, and downlights can be dimmed manually, and there is a separate switching for the uplights. This flexible system can create variations of intimacy and loftiness, with illumination from selective to full.

The previous system consumed 9,000 watts; it provided eight to ten foot-candles to the pews, and no light at all to the ceiling. The new system uses 6,000 watts and, when all the lights are operating at maximum intensity, provides about 32 foot-candles at the pews. The dimming feature makes for long lamp life, as well as variable kinds of ambiance.

The total project came in under budget which naturally pleased the parishioners. Their greatest pleasure, however, is the effect on their windows. For the first time in the 42-year history of the church, the stained-glass windows can be seen from the outside at night.

project   **St. Stephen's Church**
          Belvedere, CA
lighting **Randall Whitehead**
architect **Harold Hansen**
photographer **Ben Janken**

Custom wall sconces, lamped with compact metal halide
sources pointed upward, and color-corrected incandescent
R40 lamps pointed downward, create a dramatic, yet
humanizing overall effect.

project **St. Stephen's Church Belvedere, CA**
lighting **Randall Whitehead**
architect **Harold Hansen**
photographer **Ben Janken**

The metal halide lamps inside the sconces do an excellent job of showing off the ceiling details and providing a crisp overall illumination.

h o u s e s   o f
w o r s h i p

project **Durham Cathedral England, UK**
lighting **Graham Phoenix**
architect **Ian Curry**
photographer **Chris Arthur**

Lighting of the choir showing the highlighting of the Neville screen behind the high altar.

project **Durham Cathedral England, UK**
lighting **Graham Phoenix**
architect **Ian Curry**
photographer **Chris Arthur**

The scheme comprises a large number of projectors mounted in the galleries, using mainly 300-watt tungsten halogen sources with a choice of five different lenses, varying from very narrow to very wide. Downlighting on the pews provides the practical illumination. This is balanced by the high-lighting of the architecture including the face of the triforium and the main piers of the arcade.

project   **Durham Cathedral**
                England, UK
lighting   **Graham Phoenix**
architect   **Ian Curry**
photographer   **Chris Arthur**

The creation of mutiple lighting elements enables the
cathedral to be presented and experienced under
many different lighting conditions. The lighting control
system employs techniques similar to those used in
stage lighting. Control is achieved through the use of
dimmers and a computer-based control with
pre-programmed scenes. The system allows the full
cathedral to be lit for grand services, or the choir
area alone may be lit for smaller, evening functions.

project	**Church of Our Lady of Loretto**
	Notre Dame, IN
lighting	**William C. Lam**
architect	**Woollen, Molzan and Partners, Inc.**
interior	**Woollen, Molzan and Partners, Inc.**
photographer	**Balthazar Korab**

A transparent acoustical reflector in the Church of Our Lady of Loretto at Notre Dame is used to integrate the lighting and sound systems. It allows lighting scenes to be created for different liturgical events.

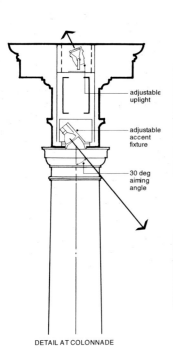

adjustable uplight

adjustable accent fixture

30 deg aiming angle

DETAIL AT COLONNADE

[left] In addition to lighting attached to the new acoustical reflector, a colonnade conceals uplighting for the murals, as well as task and accent lighting for the space.

[right] Use of fixtures on this 25-foot diameter ring allows "theater in the round" lighting for events.

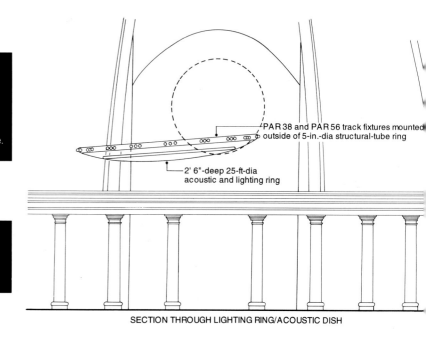

PAR 38 and PAR 56 track fixtures mounted outside of 5-in.-dia structural-tube ring

2' 6"-deep 25-ft-dia acoustic and lighting ring

SECTION THROUGH LIGHTING RING/ACOUSTIC DISH

project	**Duquette Pavillion**
	San Francisco, CA
lighting	**Tony Duquette**
architect	**Tony Duquette**
interior	**Tony Duquette**
photographer	**Douglas A. Salin**

[top] The Ducquette Pavillion is a place of magic and quiet wonder. The multi-layered lighting system adds a tremendous sense of depth to the altar area. The two green urns are illuminated from within so that the gossamer leaves glow. The metallic trees, too, have an interior illumination that energizes the senses. Theatrical fixtures hidden behind the arched proscenium do a spectacular job of bringing the sunburst to life, while hundreds of candles surround the figure of Saint John.

[bottom] Well-integrated lighting enhances the inspiring art and architectural detailing. Warm-colored lamps play up the sheen of the metal surfaces.

project
Temple Emanu El Sanctuary
San Francisco, CA
lighting
Len Auerbach, Larry French
architect
David Robinson
photographer
Bob Swanson

Surrounding the choir are large ornamental g
that frame the tabernacle area. The individua
grille sections are defined by double columns
support the arching top of each grille. Becaus
the deep relief ornamentation and gold leaf fi
the grilles are illuminated with a grazing light
emphasize the architectural shape.

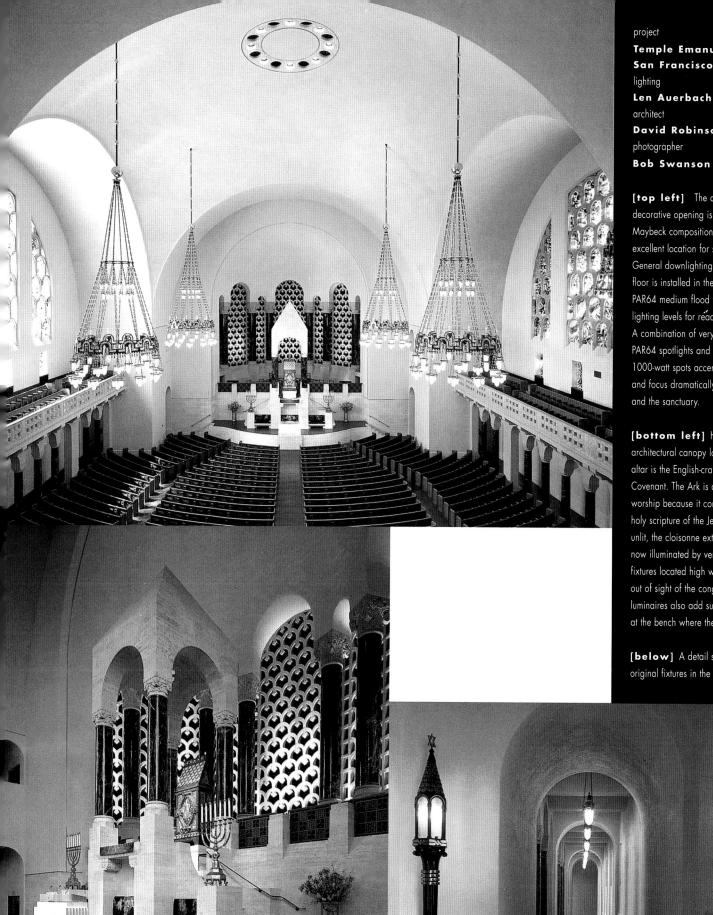

project
**Temple Emanu El Sanctuary
San Francisco, CA**
lighting
Len Auerbach, Larry French
architect
David Robinson
photographer
Bob Swanson

[top left] The design of this decorative opening is based upon an early Maybeck composition and provides an excellent location for supplemental lighting. General downlighting of the congregation floor is installed in the oculus: 1000-watt PAR64 medium flood fixtures increase lighting levels for reading prayer books. A combination of very narrow, 6-volt PAR64 spotlights and theatrical ellipsoidal 1000-watt spots accent the side altar areas and focus dramatically on the central altar and the sanctuary.

[bottom left] Housed beneath the architectural canopy located behind the altar is the English-crafted Ark of the Covenant. The Ark is a central focus of worship because it contains the Torah, the holy scripture of the Jewish faith. Previously unlit, the cloisonne exterior of the Ark is now illuminated by very small MR16 fixtures located high within the canopy and out of sight of the congregation. These luminaires also add supplemental lighting at the bench where the scriptures are read.

[below] A detail shot of the retrofitted original fixtures in the hallways.

h o u s e s   o f

w o r s h i p

project	**Basilica Nuestra Señora del Pilar Argentina**
lighting	**Leonor Bedel and Associates**
architect	**Primoli y Blanqui**
photographer	**Hector y Jorge Verdecchia**

Dimmable halogen sources were chosen for their color rendition, which complements the other, more traditional, incandescent sources in the church.

project	**Basilica Nuestra Señora del Pilar Argentina**	The Basilica Del Pilar is located in the historic district of the city.
lighting	**Leonor Bedel and Associates**	Great care was taken to install
architect	**Primoli y Blanqui**	lighting that provides adequate illumination without overpowering
photographer	**Hector y Jorge Verdecchia**	the existing decorative fixtures.

h o u s e s o f
w o r s h i p

SHOWROOMS AND DISPLAY

drawing on dynamic impact

Showrooms depend on properly designed lighting, and on creating the right atmosphere to make the merchandise or product look enticing. In a showroom, more than any other place, the lighting effects must be spectacular—patrons expect to see products presented dramatically. Thus, accent lighting takes center stage, but this does not mean that ambient lighting can be ignored: these two aspects of lighting design must blend together to create a visual balance.

The ambient lighting should be sumptuous, filling large showroom spaces with soft illumination that lets the room seem lofty without being intimidating. Very often, much of the potential drama in a grand room is missed because the architecture is not given enough emphasis by the lighting design. Well-designed lighting brings out the best aspects of a space's architectural assets. Accent lighting can then enhance those wonderful touches by adding depth, dimension, and, above all, drama.

The lighting in a showroom can be more daring than lighting in a retail space, but the essentials still remain the same: people need to be illuminated as well as architecture, and the lighting should not overpower the room. In showrooms, light must still play the role of a servant to the customers, art, and architecture, rather than that of the master, commanding all the attention.

project	**San Francisco Mart**
	San Francisco, CA
lighting	**Randall Whitehead**
architect	**Linda Hinrichs**
interior	**Linda Hinrichs**
photographer	**Donna Kempner**

Black lights punch up neon-bright colors in this surrealistic display.

project	**Pool House, San Francisco, CA**
lighting	**Becca Foster**
architect	**Steve Geiszler and Ken Rupel**
interior	**Steve Geiszler and Ken Rupel**
photographer	**Sharon Risedorph**

These fixtures have deeply saturated color filters to wash brushed-aluminum panels in bright colors. Pool luminaires were re-lamped and colored gels were added to extend the colors below water, creating the illusion that the panels continue deeply below the surface.

project
**Chrysler Technology
Center, Styling Dome
Auburn Hills, MI**
lighting
**Stefan Graf, Illuminart
Mojtaba Navaab,
University of Michigan**
architect
CRSS Architects, Inc.
interior
CRSS Architects, Inc.
photographer
Balthazar Korab

Red and blue theatrical filters, along with dichroics and gobos, can turn the simulation dome into a whirring blur of colors and shapes. The gobos also have more practical uses. Engineers can use the leaf pattern to simulate how a car looks parked under a tree, and one of the patterns is the Chrysler logo.

Chrysler Technology Center Michigan

For Chrysler's three-million square-foot Technology Center in Michigan, lighting designer Stefan Graf was faced with enormous challenges. This one-billion-dollar center for car designers, engineers, and those in charge of marketing and purchase of materials was created as the place where 7,000 employees coordinate work on design and engineering. The styling dome is the highlight of the center. The dome is a fully enclosed part of the building that can serve as a facility for company officers, a press preview area for new models, and a meeting place for directors reviewing product design.

The dome has a programmable, direct and indirect lighting system. The designers can see the new models in controlled conditions that simulate the outdoors when outdoor viewing is inhibited by weather. The dome has three turntables for display models, and an 80-foot wide projection screen that can be lowered into the floor. The dome's up-to-date acoustic features include perforated metal panels that absorb excess sound.

Naturally, lighting was a prime concern because of the huge visual impact it can have on product evaluation. This design allows for computer-controlled changes in light quality, quantity, pattern, and color.

Luminaries are installed behind 14-inch wide retractable perforated aluminum disks, placed to highlight the contours and features of cars on the floor; 85 lamps can illuminate up to 21 cars with 5600 degrees Kelvin metal halide light. The color rendering index (CRI) of this light closely approaches that of the sun.

The luminaires have motorized mirrors that allow a 360 degree rotation of the beam. Adjustments can be made in beam size, beam edge (hard or soft) and templates to create special effects patterns that simulate various shadows in outdoor lighting conditions.

Mojtaba Navvab of University of Michigan's architecture, planning, and research laboratory provided the light angles necessary for even illumination of the surface of the dome. Dome and cove walls are illuminated using a combination of compact fluorescents, metal halide, and filtered quartz lamps, located both on the floor and the top of the cove walls.

Compact fluorescent lamps illuminate the lower areas of the dome, while metal halide and quartz lamps provide light for the center and upper areas. The quartz and compact fluorescents help compensate for the metal halides' four-minute warm up time. The other lamps actually dim at the same rate that the metal halides come up, so the illumination is consistent.

project   **Chrysler Technology Center, Styling Dome**
             Auburn Hills, MI
lighting   **Stefan Graf, Illuminart**
             Mojtaba Navaab, University of Michigan
architect   **CRSS Architects, Inc.**
interior   **CRSS Architects, Inc.**
photographer **Balthazar Korab**

The styling dome is designed to allow manufacturer's engineers to see prototypes under conditions that simulate daylight as much as possible. Sky conditions are simulated by concealed light sources in two accessible perimeter coves uplighting the dome's surface. The designers specified 85 14-inch-diameter holes in the ceiling for theatrical lighting. Dichroic filters allow the reduction of the color temperature in steps from 5600 degrees Kelvin to 3000 degrees Kelvin, as required.

For indirect lighting, luminaires, and lamps used include Elliptipar with GE 40-watt 3500 degrees Kelvin biax, 350-watt HIR T-3 quartz with glass color-correction filtered and 5600 degrees Kelvin metal halide lamps. Product lighting is provided using custom luminaires with Hi End Systems GE 1200-watt M.S.R.

showrooms
and display

project   **Allrich Gallery**
                San Francisco, CA
lighting   **Becca Foster**
architect   **Suzanne Parsons**
interior   **Suzanne Parsons**
photographer   **Ken Rice**

Easy to re-lamp and maintain, energy efficient, with a constant color temperature, and high rendering capability, 60-watt and 100-watt PAR 38 Hir flood lamps are excellent choices for lighting the back of the artwork. Low-voltage recessed adjustable fixtures were installed in the niches.

project   **Allrich Gallery**
                San Francisco, CA
lighting   **Becca Foster**
architect   **Suzanne Parsons**
interior   **Suzanne Parsons**
photographer   **Ken Rice**

The track lighting installed in rectilinear configurations on the ceiling integrates well with the architecture, and provides maximum lighting flexibility for constantly changing shows.

project   **Bomani Gallery**
                San Francisco, CA
lighting   **Becca Foster**
architect   **Suzanne Parsons**
interior   **George De Witt**
photographer   **Ken Rice**

A suspended wire system with artful fixtures was installed in the entryway skylight well to keep in pace with both the contemporary furniture and the art displayed. Stunning wall-mounted articulating task luminaires are installed both at the reception desk and the owner's private office.

project
San Francisco Mart
San Francisco, CA
lighting
Randall Whitehead
architect
Andrew Batey
interior
Andrew Batey
photographer
Donna Kempner

A slowly rotating color wheel turns static nylon cord into a fantasy fountain. The task for the interior designer was to do something creative with the nylon fiber used to make carpeting, so he created a fountain. Using an ellipsoidal theatrical fixture fitted with a rotating color wheel, the lighting designer was able to give the nylon sculpture an illusion of movement.

project   **Japanese American**
           National Museum
           Los Angeles, CA
lighting   **Susan Huey and**
           Hiram Banks
interior   **Gene Takeshita**
photographer **Beatriz Coll,**
           Coll Photography

Custom low-voltage, cool-beam accent lighting, suspended from a pole-mounted cable lighting system, provides safe and soft lighting for this rare and fragile exhibit. Since this building is a historical landmark, designers were prohibited from adding new lighting on ceilings or walls, so electric power was brought up through the floor.

project   **Display Light, Carmel Valley, CA**
lighting   **Donald Maxcy**
interior   **Donald Maxcy**
photographer **Batista Moon Studio**

A suspended truss with PAR lamps provides accent and soft ambient light. The apparent source of template lighting is from the truss, but concealed higher is the gobo pattern in a theatrical luminaire. The sense of calm and quiet presence in this vignette evokes a contemplative response from viewers.

project   **San Francisco Mart**
             San Francisco, CA
lighting   **Randall Whitehead**
architect   **Andrew Batey**
interior   **Andrew Batey**
photographer **Donna Kempner**

Fashioned by architect Andrew Batey, a "dungeon" created from styrofoam allows a tiny shaft of light to illuminate its inner sanctum, one of a series of display windows created in a collaboration between designers from various fields and lighting consultant Randall Whitehead. A low-voltage PAR 36 lamp projects the tight beam of illumination, as if an unseen window allows a sliver of light to fall on the sequestered carpet.

s h o w r o o m s
a n d   d i s p l a y

project
**Knoll International
GmbH Showroom
Frankfurt, Germany**
lighting
Lighting Design Partnership
interior architect
Studios Architecture
photographer
Engelhardt and Sellin

A rough screen of 40 cm by 40 cm spruce
timbers, set like bridge trestles in a framework
of vertical and standing uprights, runs across
the back of the showroom.

project	**Toyota AMLUX Osaka Osaka, Japan**
lighting	**Kaoru Mende**
architect	**Takenaka Corporation**
interior	**Fumio Enomoto, Yasuo Kondo and Daiko Corp.**
photographer	**Nacasa and Partners, Inc.**

This floor does double duty as a reception area, and is
cross-illuminated by numerous recessed luminaires. The
area lights from the ceiling, columns, and the wall in the
back (wall washers on the aluminum wall), provide good
overall illumination.

project	**Toyota AMLUX Osaka Osaka, Japan**
lighting	**Kaoru Mende**
architect	**Takenaka Corporation**
interior	**Fumio Enomoto, Yasuo Kondo and Daiko Corp.**
photographer	**Nacasa and Partners, Inc.**

In the new Toyota AMLUX showroom in Osaka, the design
of each floor from the first to the third is based on the
concept of a building with circulating passages. A unique
louvered ceiling under the deep eaves shines with soft,
indirect light to impress visitors. Halogen lamps add
sparkling effects, creating an even more dramatic welcome.

project
United Chair Showroom
New York City, NY
lighting
Steven Bliss,
T. Kondos Associates
interior
Tom Gass, Gass Design
photographer
Peter Paige

[right] Double-hung gathered sheers are illuminated by adjustable lamps suspended on cables from the slab above, and weighted by black spheres. The electrical cords hang loose and recess at the floor level through cutout mouse holes. This also allows air conditioning to flow from window wall to showroom. At full light level, the sheers become opaque; when dimmed, they become translucent and reveal the entire chair collection.

[bottom right] This conference table is lit by a recessed quarts floodlight installed in its base, which illuminates a suspended white disc overhead.

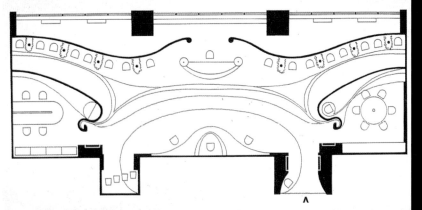

[diagram] Here, the lighting design challenge was to transform a nondescript, rectangular office space into a visually enticing contract chair showroom that would attract customers. In addition, the client needed areas to display a 30-product collection in its entirety, along with areas for reception, private conferences, work, and storage.

project **Amoco Fabric
and Fibers Company
Atlanta, GA**
lighting **Gandy/ Peace, Inc.**
interior **Gandy/ Peace, Inc.**
photographer **Chris A. Little**

The flexibility of Power trac lighting works well to enhance changing displays, and also illuminates movable Tiffany-style display windows.

project **Yarn Company
Showroom
Atlanta, GA**
lighting **Gandy / Peace, Inc.**
interior **Gandy / Peace, Inc.**
photographer **Chris A. Little**

[left] The drama created by this black space with its theatrical lighting caused record numbers of show attendees to stop and visit, thus introducing a new product to hundreds of people.

[below] The concept behind this 5,000-square-foot temporary showroom for a major yarn manufacturer was to provide a dramatic and simple space for seminars and cocktail parties, and to highlight and introduce new product information (coordinated with the overall advertising theme of "Leading the Revolution"). Simple, unobtrusive track lighting and "shop" fixtures provide flexible, economical, and effective fill and focus light.

project   **Lackawana Leather Showroom
Chicago, IL**
lighting   **Len Auerbach and Patricia Glasow**
architect   **Andrew Belschner and Joseph Vincent**
photographer   **Nick Merrick**

Custom adjustable armatures holding MR11 spot lamps graze the front of each hanging leather panel with light. Reflective metal squares on the floor, and mirrors on the wall behind the panels, scatter light around the room so additional fixtures are not needed to illuminate the back of the panels. Each leather panel is motorized to turn 360 degrees and is connected to a theatrical lighting control console, which programs the movement. Standard MR16 track fixtures with 50-watt flood lamps are used to illuminate the entry, leather drapery, and leather panel wall.

project   **Amoco Fabric
and Fibers Company
Atlanta, GA**
lighting   **Gandy/ Peace, Inc.**
interior   **Gandy/ Peace, Inc.**
photographer   **Chris A. Little**

The adjustable, low-voltage downlights in the vaulted ceiling provide quality lighting and contribute to the overall drama of this showroom. A dimmer system makes it easy to change the lighting for audio-visual presentations, which are essential program requirements of the showroom.

BARS, CLUBS AND ' CAFES

intimate meeting places

Taverns, roadhouses, lounges, brew pubs, bars, and clubs— from ultra-classy to super funky—can take a dizzying variety of forms. Design is everything in these settings, as the mood is set by the surroundings. Happy, festive places evoke camaraderie. A quiet, sumptuous atmosphere creates a sense of intimacy and romance.

Lighting in bars and clubs can vary in the extreme.

Here, the designers can let their fantasy visions run wild, and the rules of lighting, such as foot candles and color temperature, become more flexible. No longer utilitarian, lighting in these settings becomes part of the pizazz.

In lighting bars and clubs, designers have discovered a myriad of non-traditional uses for traditional fixtures. Even the low-tech lava lamp finds new life as a design

component on huge outer-space-inspired luminaires. There is a great deal of freedom in creating designs for bars and clubs. Since each club vies with the next for patrons, the keynote of lighting clubs is drama. Functionality and flattering fill light take a back seat to mood lighting and flashy special effects. People long for an escape, even if it is just for a few hours. These

establishments can be a welcome oasis.

project
Mud Bug OTB
Chicago, IL
lighting
Aumiller Youngquist, P.C.
architect
Aumiller Youngquist, P.C.
interior
Aumiller Youngquist, P.C.
photographer
Tim Long Photography

A shot of the street elevation showing the cafe entry on the left and the old loading dock on the right. Blue neon letters highlight the no-nonsense exterior. The tower is visible from nearby North Avenue, a main thoroughfare.

project	**Mud Bug OTB**
	Chicago, IL
lighting	**Aumiller Youngquist, P.C.**
architect	**Aumiller Youngquist, P.C.**
interior	**Aumiller Youngquist, P.C.**
photographer	**Tim Long Photography**

A view of the main bar showing an artifact bartap and betting counters in the background. Abundant downlighting lets customers play without distraction.

project	**Caroline's Comedy Club** **New York, NY**
lighting	**Paul Haigh**
architect	**Haigh.Architects.Designers**
interior	**Paul Haigh,** **Barbara H. Haigh**
photographer	**Elliot Kaufman**

[above] The seating tiers of the club are accented with fiber optics and the "Caroline's" sign is highlighted with three-color bank lights.

[above] This detail view of the drinks rail at the rear of the theatre shows an uplight projection onto the concrete wall.

[below] This view of the free-standing bar tables, positioned below recessed downlights, shows the elliptical shape of the stone table tops projected onto the terrazzo floor.

Caroline's Comedy Nightclub New York City New York

When Caroline's Comedy Nightclub moved to Broadway in New York City and increased in size, the new space was totally revamped to match the style that owner Caroline Hirsch felt was required. The new space was huge and quite intimidating. The design objective was to create a club large enough to be profitable, but also to include more intimate areas where patrons could congregate in comfort.

Besides the main theater section, a bar area that also serves as a place for people to wait before shows was incorporated into the design.

Designers Paul and Barbara Haigh's aim was to fulfill these functions while retaining a sense of comfort in the vast space. They chose the atmosphere of a medieval fair as a theme for decor, using a harlequin pattern on birch plywood, velvets, and tapestries. Colorful banquettes provide some of the seating for the diners, and the harlequin pattern is carried throughout the club on tabletops, doors, the face of the bar, and carpets. Uplighting on the drink rails adds to the dazzling look.

Fiber optics outline various architectural features, to help patrons find their way through the club. Tiny incandescent lamps with shades dot the tables, creating inviting places to gather. Low-voltage, recessed, MR16 downlights highlight the bar tables, and recessed floor fixtures illuminate the wall and additional bar seating areas. Fiber-optic lights on the top of banquettes add color (two 150-watt metal halide illuminators use color wheels to vary the fiber optic lighting) and detail to the design. Velvet-paneled draperies, illuminated with the narrow spotlights of low-voltage, surface-mounted fixtures, help soften the feel of the space and allow different levels to be closed off, depending on crowd size.

Over the bar, half-inch fiber-optics on the soffit change color from magenta to aqua to green to white, with remote-controlled metal halide illuminators providing the main light source. Recessed fixtures with PAR36 narrow spots over fiber optics help light areas near the bar. These can be redirected as necessary.

For the theater, the unfinished concrete rear wall is uplit to highlight its unusual texture. Uplighting is also used to enhance tempered glass shelves along the bar's back wall. Lumiere outdoor fixtures, (they are actually swimming pool lights), recessed into the floor and lensed in different colors, cast interesting shadows on the walls, shelving, and drinks resting on the bar. Eleven banks of wall washers, housing nine 150-watt R40 lamps, each contain red, green, and blue lights that can be combined to make a variety of colors.

Caroline's is dramatic in more than just decor and lighting; the club is often used for television broadcasts. Because of this, versatility is built into the complex lighting systems of the space. A 48-patch Entertainer lighting console is preset to provide different backdrops for broadcasts. Architectural lighting uses a Versaplex system from Lutron.

From lounge to stairway to stage, Caroline's successfully integrates functional lighting design with a grand sense of theater.

project
**Caroline's Comedy Club
New York, NY**
lighting
Paul Haigh
architect
Haigh.Architects.Designers
interior
**Paul Haigh,
Barbara H. Haigh**
photographer
Elliot Kaufman

A detail view of main bar showing barfly stools. The glass soffit is downlit with recessed MR16 halogen lamps. The bar fascia is washed with light from fiberoptics. The back bar display is highlighted with recessed lights.

[inset] This view of the main bar/lounge shows the highlighted seating and dining areas. A curved architectural soffit is delineated with fiber-optic strings.

project
Velfarre
Tokyo, Japan
lighting
Stom Ushidate
architect
Robert R. Lowe
interior
Stom Ushidate
photographer
Nacasa & Partners Inc.

High-tech "monitor" wall sconces
and red spotlights set the mood in
this club lobby.

project
Velfarre
Tokyo, Japan
lighting
Stom Ushidate
architect
Robert R. Lowe
interior
Stom Ushidate
photographer
Nacasa & Partners Inc.

Custom-curved hood lights enhance the illusion of floating in space. The blue color of the hoods is highlighted with small aperture fixtures mounted in the ceiling.

b a r s ,

c l u b s ,

a n d

c a f e s

project
Velfarre
Tokyo, Japan
lighting
Stom Ushidate
architect
Robert R. Lowe
interior
Stom Ushidate
photographer
Nacasa & Partners Inc.

A spectacular shot of the reception area looking up from feature staircase. The designers used cracked glass and edge lighting to create an image of fantasy and the illusion of instability.

project **MG Planet**
Tokyo, Japan
lighting **TL Yamagiwa Laboratory**
interior **Masanori Umeda**
photographer **Yoshio Shiratori**

A stainless-steel wire grid creates a boundary between the restaurant's actual space and the fantastical illusion of cosmic space expanding above the patrons. Thousands of miniature electric bulbs become a universe, thanks to mirrors on the surrounding walls.

b a r s ,
c l u b s ,
a n d
c a f e s

project **Yoshida Bar**
Tokyo, Japan
lighting **Yukio Oka**
interior **Keizo Okazaki**
photographer **Atelier Fukumoto**

[above] Ambient lighting is provided by a sleek back-lit soffit, which gives the space a lush, comfortable atmosphere. Sandblasted glass bowls are suspended from the ceiling by nearly invisible stainless steel wire.

[left] Recessed downlights providing the illumination make these glass bowls seem to float on air, and cast diffused light over the bar counter. Glowing "brackets" appear to be helping hold up the ceiling with the strength of light itself. To create a perfect balance, all of the lights are controlled by dimmers.

project	**MG Planet**
	Tokyo, Japan
lighting	**TL Yamagiwa Laboratory**
interior	**Masanori Umeda**
photographer	**Yoshio Shiratori**

MG Planet attracts clientele from the fields of advertising and journalism. The "science fiction" atmosphere suggests that patrons are visiting from other planets to enjoy "earth" food, music, and drinks.

217

project
America's Restaurant
Houston, TX
lighting
Jordan Mozer
architect
Larry Traxler
interior
Jordan Mozer
photographer
David Clifton

A pre-Columbian theme is carried through the design of this restaurant, from architecture to artifacts. Here, the very walls resemble woven cloth and the pendants resemble some ancient Mayan or Inca symbol. These fantastic ceiling fixtures and wall sconces are made of painted, hand-cut aluminum and blown glass.

project
Surf 'n' Turf
Matsuyama, Japan
lighting
Jordan Mozer
architect
Jordan Mozer
interior
Jordan Mozer
photographer
Take Ichi

This dining area is lit by glowing horns and sea-creature pendants. The walls bulge, and even the chairs join in the weird panorama.

project
Iridium
New York, NY
lighting
Jordan Mozer
architect
Jeff Carloss
interior
Jordan Mozer
photographer
Andrew Garn

For Iridium, the designers sought to infuse the space with the spirit of a dream or a poem: this nightspot is never what you expect, forms twist and curve in astonishing ways and the soft lighting brings out the startling effects.

project
Surf 'n' Turf
Matsuyama, Japan
lighting
Jordan Mozer
architect
Jordan Mozer
interior
Jordan Mozer
photographer
Take Ichi

Fantasy dream pendants, with glass tentacles as if from sea creatures, provide glowing, ambient light, and create a setting that surprises the senses.

project	**Stars California Restaurant**
	Frankfurt, Germany
lighting	**Jordan Mozer**
architect	**Jordan Mozer**
interior	**Jordan Mozer**
photographer	**Helmut Mitter**

Blown glass inserted into the tops of decorative columns conveys a feeling of pulsing matter and energy. Flowing star-like shapes on the wall add to the effect.

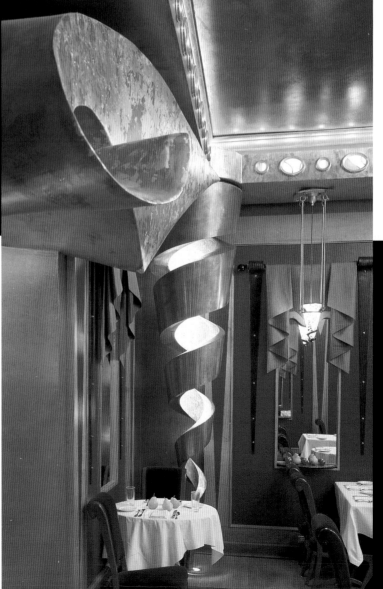

project
Vivere
Chicago, IL
lighting
Jordan Mozer
architect
Jordan Mozer
interior
Jordan Mozer
photographer
David Clifton

For Vivere, the designer looked to the spirals of Italian baroque architecture for inspiration. The tables are surrounded by spiral shapes, and a wall spiral is lit from within. Softly burnished gilt finishes reflect ambient light with an amber glow.

project **BACK LOT**
of the After Dark
Monterey, CA
lighting **Donald Maxcy**
architect **Donald Maxcy**
photographer **Russell Abraham**

Light draws the eye inside this sumptuous back bar. Mirrors enlarge the visual volume of the room and help bounce light around in the space. Chunks of glass block, glued together with silicone instead of mortar, are playfully reminiscent of ice cubes. The low-tech lights within the blocks are dimmable.

project **Harlands**
Fresno, CA
lighting **Donald Maxcy**
architect **Kennedy Lutz**
Architecture
interior **Charles Grebmeier**
photographer **Russell Abraham**

Lighting becomes artwork in this project. Subtle colored gels were used behind glass-block chair rails and block windows. A suspended low-voltage track system brings light down into the dining space and counter areas. The floating serpentine elements conceal lighting over the bar.

b a r s ,
c l u b s ,
a n d
c a f e s

project **The Sound Factory**
San Francisco, CA
lighting **Terry Ohm**
photographer **Charles Cormany**

For the large dance room in this 20,000-square foot nightclub, 16 High End Systems Trackspots are suspended from a custom bracket, giving the illusion that the fixtures are floating in the air. A fully programmable robotic fixture, the Trackspot offers color changing, color mixing, movement, and pattern projection. The dance room also contains a Diversitronic strobe system, laser stimulators, and a fogger system.

THEATERS AND MOVIE HOUSES

s e t t i n g   t h e   m o o d

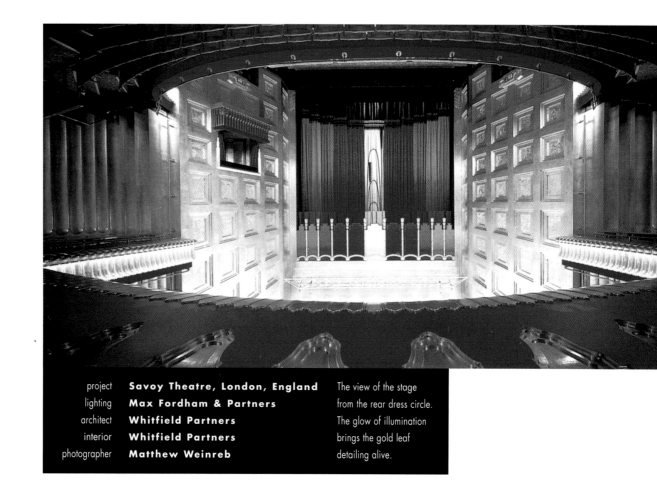

project	**Savoy Theatre, London, England**	The view of the stage
lighting	**Max Fordham & Partners**	from the rear dress circle.
architect	**Whitfield Partners**	The glow of illumination
interior	**Whitfield Partners**	brings the gold leaf
photographer	**Matthew Weinreb**	detailing alive.

Most of us thought that the dramatic, elegant movie palaces and theaters of the past were gone, with unimaginative multiplexes— no more than a series of boxes—left in their places. Well, what was lost is found again in a whole new generation of deluxe movie emporiums and dramatic theaters. Along with the newly-built are sumptuously remodeled and restored gems from our collective past.

Once again, the theater-going experience begins with the first glimpse of a brightly lit marquee, and continues into the lobby. The magic of movies and of live theater, much to the delight of the public, is spilling over into its environment. The best new lighting designs for theaters and movie houses enhance both restored period features and futuristic surfaces, lending a "larger than life" feeling to the interior surroundings.

Since the advent of video, which digs into movie revenues each time theater-goers choose to watch at home, the film industry has begun to take a hard look at where films are shown. To compete, the industry is striving to transform the movie-going experience back into something special. Lighting is an integral part of that change, and the new lighting methods work to create dynamic effects in the movie house, as well as on the movie screen.

project	**Savoy Theatre, London, England**
lighting	**Max Fordham & Partners**
architect	**Whitfield Partners**
interior	**Whitfield Partners**
photographer	**Matthew Weinreb**

Viewed from the circle of the proscenium arch panel, stage lighting within the coffer blends with the architecture.

project
**John L. Tishman
Auditorium
New School
for Social Research,
New York, NY**
lighting
Frank Kelly
architect
**Rolf Olhausen, Principal
Barbara Spandorf
Architects, Inc.**
interior
**Rolf Olhausen, Principal
Barbara Spandorf**
photographer
Brian Rose

Stage lighting was removed from the flanking arcades, which had never provided light from the proper angles. Some mounted fixtures were added on ladders at the back of the balcony, on either side of the projection booth. The most visible ones seem to slip discreetly from the shadows of one of the ceiling tiers; they can be lowered for maintenance and unplugged completely for events that call for showing the architectural purity of the space. Meanwhile, the arcades are free to celebrate themselves in the gleam of concealed downlights. A single control system operates architectural presets and a theatrical console.

John L. Tishman Auditorium New School for Social Research New York City New York

For many years, the lighting for the Tishman Auditorium at the New School for Social Research had provided both too much light and too little. Though the people on stage were overwhelmed by the glare, paradoxically, they still lacked good enough reading light for notes or scores. The subtle grays of the room had long given way to plain white. Much of the original design of the space had been changed, and its original atmosphere was totally lost.

Three years ago, the auditorium was restored to its original colors and given an expanded stage, refurbished furniture, and additional modern technical systems, as well as acoustical improvements. New lighting was designed as if the original architect, Joseph Urban, had been given access to today's technology when the auditorium was built in the thirties. Architect Rolf Ohlhausen, of Prentice and Chan, Olhausen Architects worked with lighting designer Frank Kelly, of Imero Fiorentino Associates, to restore the truly modern concept of the space.

Original cove lighting is retained in the upper tiers, but, for energy efficiency that does not sacrifice effect, halogen lamps replace standard incandescents. The intended gray shades of the interior are also restored, and benefit from the improved color rendering of the lighting. Permanent downlights on stage provide good reading light for performers. The overall stage lighting is greatly improved by the addition of QPAR 56 lights in concealed ceiling coves, ellipsoidal reflector spotlights on motorized lighting pipes flanking the stage, and ladder-mounted fixtures at the back of the balcony.

In the armrests of the seating, low-voltage strip lights illuminate the way for audience members. Above the doors, new soffits accommodate exit signs and emergency lighting.

General illumination is improved by recessed QPAR 56 adjustable downlights, which are adjacent to the original, luminous white glass panels that once provided most of the general light. A new, combination architectural/theatrical dimming system makes the auditorium more flexible with push-button preset stations for general classroom use and a memory console for theatrical performances.

In the lobby, the lighting is completely redone; recessed, compact fluorescent emergency lights replace one-by four-foot surface-mounted strips, and a flexible, compact fluorescent strip takes over for the ceiling cove's outmoded incandescent socket strips. Last, the new lighting's color temperature is 3500 degrees Kelvin carefully chosen to blend well with the abundant daylight spilling in through the auditorium's glass doors.

project
**John L. Tishman
Auditorium
New School for Social
Research, New York, NY**
lighting
Frank Kelly
architect
**Rolf Olhausen, Principal
Barbara Spandorf
Architects, Inc.**
interior
**Rolf Olhausen, Principal
Barbara Spandorf**
photographer
Brian Rose

In this auditorium's up-to-date lighting design, cove lighting repeats the flooring pattern in the lobby. Probably originally lit with strips of incandescents, the shapely cove recently sported surface-mounted fluorescent tubes before being restored to its intended color rendition with the use of compact fluorescents.

project **Sony Theatres**
New York, NY
lighting **Gallegos Lighting Design**
architect **Gensler & Associates**
interior **Gensler & Associates**
photographer **Marco Lorenzetti**

[above left] In the auditorium, wall sconces and architectural details enhance the Art Deco flavor. The indirect lighting is a refreshing change from the typical sea of downlights so often seen in multiplexes of this type.

[above] Searchlights reach for the stars to create an opening-night effect in the auditorium.

[left] In the main concessions hall, columns display timelines of the history of film development. A grove of ebony palms holds monitors that display current and future attractions.

project	**Princess of Wales Theater Ontario, Canada**
lighting	**Wallace G. Eley and D.R. Waite**
architect	**Peter Smith**
interior	**George Yabu**
photographer	**Robert Burley**

To illuminate a painting by Stella, this system of 3500 degrees Kelvin, white triphosphor, cold-cathode tubing in a preformed dome was chosen for its excellent color-rendering properties and dimming flexibility.

For aesthetic effect and definition, a line of clear lamps, dimmed to 50 percent for long life, is installed to form a trapezoidal ring at the base of the dome. This also makes maintenance easy. The upper part of the dome is surrounded with a series of PAR 20 halogen lamps.

project
**Princess of Wales Theater
Ontario, Canada**
lighting
Wallace G. Eley and D.R. Waite
architect
Peter Smith
interior
George Yabu
photographer
Robert Burley

A system of coves with 60-watt A lamps on
16-inch centers over the balcony, dress circle, and
orchestra level seating was installed to provide the
indirect lighting.

project	**Fitzgerald Theater, St. Paul, MN**
lighting	**Duane Schuler**
architect	**Miller Hanson Westerbeck Berger, Inc.**
photographer	**George Heinrich**

Custom decorative sconces, with dimmed incandescent lamps, were added
to this auditorium's side walls at all balcony and box levels. Downlights are
placed in the ceiling at locations that allow them to be re-lamped from above
via catwalks. On the stage, a new orchestra shell contains downlights
with halogen PAR 64 lamps to provide approximately 80 foot-candles of
illumination. In addition, new theatrical lighting locations were added to the
audience boxes and on the faces of the balconies.

theaters
and movie
houses

project **Sony Theatres**
New York, NY
lighting **Gallegos Lighting Design**
architect **Gensler & Associates**
interior **Gensler & Associates**
photographer **Marco Lorenzetti**

[right] This wonderful mural is a collage of the great entry marquees from Sony Theaters. The excitement of the space is enhanced by the sweeping city views, the movement of multiple escalators, and the colorful drama of the artwork. The mural is illuminated using theater luminaires mounted near the top of the columns.

[below] Sony Pictures Entertainment's new complex near Lincoln Center is the flagship for its cinema operations, as well as its premiere theater. The dynamic entry uses richly colored signage and interior lighting to create an enticing look.

[below right] This concessions stand entrance is a replica of the entry gate at Sony's main lot in Culver City, California. While recalling the past, the stand incorporates lush, modern bands of neon color overhead.

theaters and movie houses

GUEST SERVICE

project **Glyndebourne Opera House**
Lewes, East Sussex, England
lighting **George Sexton**
architect **Michael Hopkins,**
Patty Hopkins and Robin Snell
photographer **Richard Davies**

Custom, curved architectural slots at the perimeter walls house an incandescent strip light system, which washes the wood paneling and gives the theatre a stunning glow. Shallow concrete coffers are fitted with miniature incandescent light sources to provide a halo of ambient light. A series of miniature downlights, integrated into the modulating ceiling bands, cast a glow of light onto the seats and add to the "sky of stars" seen across the theatre. In addition, theatrical PAR 56 fixtures suspended from the central lighting bridge, highlight the balconies.

project **Sendai Shi Bunka Center**
Tokyo, Japan
lighting **TL Yamagiwa Laboratory**
architect **Yamashita Sekkei Inc.**
photographer **Yamagiwa Corporation**

The stage of this concert hall is illuminated with recessed downlight fixtures and recessed lights diffused by glittering light reflectors. The suspended sound reflector is height-adjustable to fit each program, its sparkling look is created by a downlight in the ceiling.

theaters
and movie
houses

project **Seafort Square Theater**
Tokyo, Japan
lighting **Shunji Tamai**
architect **RIA Company, Ltd.**
interior **RIA Company, Ltd.**
photographer **Courtesy of Shunji Tamai**

This side view of the auditorium shows the custom-mounted luminaires. Recessed fixtures provide additional light.

project	**Skylight Opera Theater**
	Milwaukee, WI
lighting	**Robert Shook and Duane Schuler**
architect	**Sherrill Myers**
interior	**David Birn and David Zinn**
photographer	**Mark Gubin**

The lighting design for the auditorium combines exposed lamp sources and hidden sources to enhance the theatrical painting and provide an inviting atmosphere for patrons. The central chandelier and the sconces at the gallery faces provide the focal points of light. Recessed downlights in the galleries and uplights onto the ceiling reveal the painted surfaces. All sources are dimmed incandescent, to meet the criteria for opera performances and to increase lamp life. Theatrical lighting for the stage is integrated into the box openings near the stage, on railings at the gallery faces, and at a fourth-floor technical gallery, painted to resemble the seating galleries below.

project
Private Theater
architect
**Backen Arrigoni and
Ross Architects**
photographer
Douglas A. Salin

This lush setting for private viewings
has all the advantages of a large-scale
theater, with the intimacy of a more
compact setting. Low-profile recessed
lighting brings up the sheen of
upholstery. A well-planned dimming
system allows for a classroom setting,
as well as comfortable movie-watching.

project
**Boehringer Ingelheim
Pharmaceuticals
Richfield, CT**
lighting
Childs & Scolze
architect
Gensler & Associates
interior
Gensler & Associates
photographer
Marco Lorenzetti

Wall-washing light adds drama to a
grid-patterned wall.

project   **Yerba Buena Gardens
               Visual Arts Center
               San Francisco, CA**
lighting   **Patricia Glasow, Len Auerbach,
               Principal Mark Rudiqer**
architect   **Maki and Associates
               Robinson, Mills + Williams**
photographer   **John Barnes Photography**

The Forum, a flexible theatrical
space, incorporates three
complete lighting systems:
theatrical performance lighting,
tungsten halogen downlighting
for performances and parties,
and metal halide downlighting
for brightly lit activities.

project
**Alcazar Theater
San Francisco, CA**
interior lighting
David Ebert
exterior lighting
Teal Brogden
architect
Bill Pearson
interior
David Ebert
photographer
Robert Swanson

[left] The style of this eclectic building is Moorish and Byzantine. The exterior materials are glazed terra cotta tile, and brick, with marble panels at the entrance, and recessed stucco walls. Strategically placed uplighting throws fanciful architectural detail into theatrical relief.

[below left] Original interior embellishment of the theater is modest, limited to the main entrance and assembly areas. Cove lighting in the entryway creates an enticing air of mystery. Deeply recessed "star" windows, illuminated from within, cast dramatic, sculptural shadows.

OFFICE SPACES

chapter eight

Office environments are reaching new levels of comfort. Today, the cold, almost clinical spaces of traditional office design have given way to a more residential style. A greater use of texture and color by interior designers and architects is being combined with a new approach to corporate lighting. Standard office lighting design once consisted of two- by four-foot recessed fluorescent fixtures suspended in a ceiling grid. This made

for a work environment filled with a harsh, somewhat depressing light. The first step toward changing this practice came with the introduction of indirect light sources that bounced light off the ceiling to create a soft overall glow. Since this method, by itself, still looks flat, decorative fixtures and accent lights are now added to provide visual

interest and sparkle.

The color quality of fluorescents and high-intensity discharge sources has also improved. In addition, ultra-quiet, solid-state ballasts and very compact light sources allow for a much more friendly use of energy-efficient lamps. In planning office lighting schemes, the challenge is to be creative

and energy-concious at the same time. The realities of energy regulations do not have to dampen the spirit of good design: many of the projects featured in this chapter don't resemble traditional offices at all. Their success demonstrates how greatly office spaces have changed for the better in just the last few years.

project	**The Port of Oakland Oakland, CA**
lighting	**Horton Lees Lighting**
architect	**Robinson Mills + Williams**
interior	**Robinson Mills + Williams**
photographer	**Bob Swanson**

The expansive wood conference table provides a warm visual anchor to this voluminous conference room. Recessed low-voltage downlights enhance the color of the table while clean-lined wall sconces bounce amber light off the barrel-vault ceiling.

project **Epic Records**
Santa Monica, CA
lighting **Cosimo Pizzulli**
architect **Cosimo Pizzulli**
interior **Cosimo Pizzulli**
photographer **Fashid Assassi**

Suspended "floating cloud" ceilings cover approximately
51 percent of this open area with 1.5-inch-thick fiberglass.
The fiberglass material helps reflect ambient lighting within

Gore-Tex Japan Setagaya Tokyo

Gore-Tex, a famous manufacturer of synthetic fiber products, uses "Be Creative" as a corporate motto. Interior designer Masanori Umeda, along with lighting design by Ushiospax, sought to meet that challenge. They created an exciting design that makes the Gore-Tex space much more than an ordinary office environment, and conveys a feeling of the great outdoors.

The entrance hall features a huge, fiber-optic world map. Indirect ambient light comes from compact metal halide lamps reflecting light off the ceiling. The walls on the first floor are aluminum, silk-screened with a pattern of Gore-Tex fiber. The lighting design purposely keeps the office entrance very bright during daylight hours, with diminishing lighting as one progresses through the building, to give the eyes a chance to adjust naturally from daylight to interior light.

The lobby and meeting area evoke the panorama of the Mongolian plains, with cloud-like sculptural forms hanging over the area. Luminaires, using halogen lamps, filtered through blue films and prisms, provide the overall punch light. A circular screen of a lightly finished polycarbonate hints at the shape of a Pao, the Mongolian moveable house.

In the lounge, round anodized titanium bars reflect rainbow colors to create a wonderful screen. The bar counter is constructed of natural materials, making a forest-like setting for eating and drinking. Accent lights tucked between the ceiling beams highlight the table tops and bar surface. Mini-halogen lamps mounted on the stool legs light up the circular base panels.

This delightful combination of varied lighting, wood finishes, and imaginatively colored metals brings a needed warmth to the interiors of this large corporation.

project
Gore-Tex Japan Setagaya, Tokyo
lighting
Ushiospax
architect
Sato Kogyo
interior
Masanori Umeda
photographer
Yoshio Shiratori

On the wall by the reception counter, a world map indicates the locations of Gore-Tex branches with red, fiber-optic lights. Basic lighting is indirect but bright, using compact metal halide sources. The walls at the ground floor are aluminum, silk screened with the pattern of Gore-Tex fiber.

project
**Gore-Tex Japan
Setagaya, Tokyo**
lighting
Ushiospax
architect
Sato Kogyo
interior
Masanori Umeda
photographer
Yoshio Shiratori

[top]
The titanium bar area is anodized to show beautiful rainbow colors, and emphasized with halogen spotlights. The intended effect is that of a forest glade.

[bottom]
This space is designed to evoke the Mongolian plains. Below the ceiling, cut-outs represent a sea of clouds. Accent lights fitted with blue filters and prisms help punctuate the space. The circular screen is made of polycarbonate and hints at the image of a Pao, the Mongolian movable house.

project
**AT&T Bay Area
Special Services
Center
Oakland, CA**
lighting
**Randall Whitehead
and Catherine Ng**
architect
**John Lum,
Mike Beam, Reid &
Tarics Associates**
interior
**John Lum,
Mike Beam, Reid &
Tarics Associates**
photographer
Christopher Irion

The plans for AT&T's Bay Area
Special Services Center called for
a playful space. Saddled with the
tight wattage constrictions of
California's Title 24 energy code,
the lighting design team employed
fluorescent and high-intensity
discharge sources in creative
ways. At the entryway, workers
and visitors are greeted by a
huge cantilevered steel wall.
This imposing facade is lit from
beneath with a rosy pink neon,
which reflects off the terrazzo
floor. Lensed fluorescent wall
washers cast a similar hue on
wedge-shaped wing walls.

project
**Jack Morton
Productions
San Francisco, CA**
lighting
Susan Huey, LIT
architect
Interior Architects
interior
Interior Architects
photographer
Beatriz Coll

To maintain the open ceiling and
exposed truss architecture, the
lighting design team specified a
suspended cable-lighting system
to provide ambient light for the
table and presentation wall.

project	**Apple Computer, Inc.**
	Research and Development Campus
	Building 2
	Cupertino, CA
lighting	**S. Leonard Aurbach Associates**
architect	**HOK**
interior architect	**Studios Architecture**
photographer	**Mark Darley**

The user groups in Building Two work building-wide, but are distributed locally into workteams. They requested large central "User Defined Areas," so that members of each group would run across colleagues working far away. Frosted glass walls allow light to be shared between spaces. Whimsical pendants provide abundant light with a playful touch.

office spaces

project **Latham & Watkins**
San Francisco, CA
lighting **S. Leonard Auerbach**
& Associates
architect **Babey Moulton, Inc.**
interior **Babey Moulton, Inc.**
photographer **Nick Merrick**

The gallery and pre-function conference zone of this office has abundant daylight at the two narrow ends of a rectangular space. The natural light is balanced with recessed incandescent downlights and wall washers, to highlight a collection of photographs.

o f f i c e

s p a c e s

project **Young & Rubicam**
San Francisco, CA
lighting **Richard Hannum**
architect **Hannum Associates**
interior **Richard Hannum**
photographer **Christopher Irion**

In this law office, a barrel vault is illuminated with twin light strips recessed into a cove. Arches are backlighted with 60-watt lamps mounted behind custom, perforated metal screen walls. Low-voltage recessed adjustable MR16 downlights add additional illumination.

project **Bank of America**
San Francisco, CA
lighting **Hiram Banks, LIT**
architect **Interior Architects**
interior **Interior Architects**
photographer **Beatriz Coll**

Specially mounted low-voltage track fixtures highlight the artwork, while staggered trimline fluorescent fixtures, concealed within the architecture, provide ambient illumination.

project
**The Estate of James Campbell
Oahu, Hawaii**
lighting
Susan Huey and Hiram Banks
interior architect
Ferraro Choi and Associates, Ltd.
photographer
Jon Miller

Layers of fluorescent indirect lighting, low-voltage
task illumination, and focus lighting are combined
with palm-leaf light patterns projected on textured
walls to illuminate this corporate lobby.

project   The Estate of James Campbell
                 Oahu, Hawaii
lighting   Susan Huey and Hiram Banks
interior architect   Ferraro Choi & Associates, Ltd.
interior   Ferraro Choi and Associates, Ltd.
photographer   Jon Miller

Cobalt-blue ambient lighting complements the red LED and VDT displays of this computer center. At the touch of a button, the blue light transforms into white light for system maintenance.

project
Oracle Corporation
lighting
**James Benya,
Luminae Souter
Lighting Design**
architect
**Ehrlich Rominger
Architects**
interior
Laura Seccombe
photographer
Douglas A. Salin

The Oracle Company is a database software company located in Silicon Valley. The playful theme of the employee lunchroom gives some welcome relief from the intense work situation. The cold cathode and neon colors blend together to create a lavender glow, while the art and wall panels are punched up with a low-voltage track system using miniature mirror reflector lamps. The pendant fixtures along the back provide a sense of separation for the banquet seating.

project   **Sony Music Entertainment
                 London, UK**
lighting   **Harper Mackay Ltd.**
architect   **Harper Mackay Ltd.**
interior   **Harper Mackay Ltd.**
photographer   **Dennis Gilbert**

The high-tech look of this office cafeteria is enhanced with "floating" light planes that provide light without overpowering the space.

project
**ZD Labs, A division of
Ziff Davis Publishing
Sunnyvale, CA**
lighting
**Thomas J. Skradski,
Luminae Souter
Lighting Design**
architect
**Gene Conti and
Michael Ott**
interior
**Gene Conti and
Michael Ott**
photographer
John Sutton

This equipment testing lab required
low-level, non-glare illumination for the
technicians. The solution is a combination
of indirect wall sconces, which provide
drama and open up the dark ceiling cavity,
supported by fiber-optic tubing that outlines
the equipment racks to create a sense
of electricity. Color also plays a key role
in visually enhancing this public showcase.
In addition, louvered track lighting is used
for task light.

project
**Sony Pictures Entertainment
Los Angeles, CA**
lighting
Joe Kaplan Lighting Design
architect
Gensler & Associates
interior
Gensler & Associates
photographer
Marco Lorenzetti

Sony Theatre's new office complex near Lincoln Center serves as both the company's flagship facility, and a premiere theater. This dynamic entry incorporates an elaborate marquee and interior lighting to create an enticing look.

project	**New York State Education Building, Albany, NY**
lighting	**Bill Lam, Bob Osten and Paul Zaferiou**
architect	**Einhorn Yaffee Prescott**
interior	**Einhorn Yaffee Prescott**
photographer	**Jeff Goldberg**

These new compact fluorescent sconces mark major circulation paths and identify destinations, such as the main reception desk. Here, visible luminaires are limited to the newly constructed architectural element, which floats within the original spaces. Fluorescent uplighting concealed in the top of this element provides a soft, cheerful rendering of the vaulted shapes above. Over the original daylights, concealed metal halide downlighting supplements daylight and provides a nighttime ambient glow.

project
**Sony Music Publishing
Conference Room
Santa Monica, CA**
lighting
Cosimo Pizzulli
architect
Cosimo Pizzulli
interior
Cosimo Pizzulli
photographer
Fashid Assassi

This conference room incorporates
state-of-the-art audio-visual and
televideo conferencing controls in
the custom designed tables and
cabinetry. A CAD system was used
to plan and develop area coverage
for the acoustical system and
task/ambient lighting system.

project	**Babcock & Brown**
	San Francisco, CA
lighting	**Thomas J. Skradski,**
	Luminae Souter
architect	**Studios Architecture**
interior	**Studios Architecture**
photographer	**Paul Warchol**

The conference room is lit with a louvered low-voltage
cable system, which appears to float in front of the
panoramic view. Asymmetrical T8 fluorescent signlighters
with electronic ballasts wash the presentation walls.
The frosted-glass table top glows from louvered PAR30
halogen uplights bolted to the floor. MR16 luminaires highlight a sculptural column, enhancing its spectacular finish.

project	**The Offices of**
	Plunkett Raysich
	Milwaukee, WI
lighting	**Steven Klein,**
	Principal;
	Lana Nathe
architect	**Stephen Holzhaver**
interior	**Nancy Arriano**
photographer	**Mark Heffron**

Basic geometric shapes are the design motif of
the pendants in the main conference room.
The presentation board wall is defined by cone
aperture wallwashers with MR16 lamps.

MEDICAL CARE FACILITIES

comfort the first priority

chapter nine

In medical care facilities, special attention must be paid to illumination, because older or unwell people are more sensitive to lighting levels and sources. Lighting must be glare free and very unobtrusive, yet must offer plenty of task illumination for medical care personnel.

Good ambient illumination is the first step; providing the necessary soft fill light to make rooms comfortable, and to help lessen any disorientation that patients may experience.

Task light must also be especially well-thought-out, since medical personnel often have urgent duties and little time to set up a sufficient light source. Patients or residents require especially good lighting in areas such as bathrooms, as their visual acuity may be impaired. As in other public spaces, accent light should be used to lead people to specific destinations—such as reception, admissions, and waiting rooms, or to help to direct people away from private or restricted areas.

Good design, with well-integrated lighting, goes a long way toward making a stay in a health care facility more pleasant. The effect of environment on health is well-known, so the designer's goal is to make the setting therapeutic, rather than stressful. To that end, the projects that follow may astound you. Never before has "light as art" become one of the healing arts.

project
Health Park Medical Center
Lee County, FL
lighting
Craig Roeder
architect
HKS Inc., Architects
interior
HKS Designcare /
Medical Space Design
photographer
Robt. Ames Cook

Theatrical metal halide fixtures, fitted with dichroic filters, project a fanciful rainbow of color on the curvilinear balconies.

project
Health Park Medical Center
Lee County, FL
lighting
Craig Roeder
architect
HKS Inc., Architects
interior
HKS Designcare /
Medical Space Design
photographer
Robt. Ames Cook

The atrium of the Health Park Hospital is washed with rainbows of light from metal-halide lamps with dichroic color filters.

247

Le Bonheur Children's Medical Center Memphis Tennessee

People who are ill or injured deserve to be surrounded by comfort and beauty. Until recently, neither hospital administrators nor hospital architects and designers gave much weight to the role of the environment in a patient's recovery. "Institutional" was the word of the day, and design formulas for such locations led to efficient, sterile, dully uniform surroundings. These days, however, competition is forcing hospitals to create friendlier spaces, to attract patients to their facilities. Designers are now able to create dramatic centers of warmth and beauty, enhanced through lighting.

Le Bonheur Children's Medical Center in Memphis exemplifies the new trend in hospital and medical facilities. Lighting designer Craig Roeder, given free rein to create beauty and comfort, has stretched lighting design to the limit. To fulfill the designer's plan, this space uses all the technology available. Stars, courtesy of fiber optics, change colors as they twinkle. In one area, neon under glass block provides waves of ever-changing color, thanks to an eight-scene dimming system. Undulating bands of neon in rainbow colors constantly move up columns.

Easy maintenance was an absolute requirement, so much of the design uses neon and cold-cathode light sources that will operate for years without maintenance. Bundles of fiber optics, also low maintenance, are glued in the ceiling drywall and connect to metal halide sources with revolving color wheels (that are easy to reach on the third floor for maintenance.)

Halogen accent lighting was installed in the low-ceiling areas, and halogen uplights illuminate the awnings. Cold-cathode light circles the foot of the columns, and the tops of columns hold cold-cathode and purple neon.

This space is truly magical; adults and children alike are drawn to the atrium to watch the slow dance of light across the interior sky.

project
Le Bonheur Children's Medical Center Memphis, TN
lighting
Craig Roeder
architect
J. Wise Smith Associates, Howard K. Smith Associates
interior
Judy Hall
photographer
Robt. Ames Cook

The "ocean floor" turns a humble tunnel into an enchanting passage. An eight-scene dimmer the designer calls a "wave machine" animates neon under the glass brick.

project · **Le Bonheur Children's Medical Center Memphis, TN**
lighting · **Craig Roeder**
architect · **J. Wise Smith Associates, Howard K. Smith Associates**
interior · **Judy Hall**
photographer · **Robt. Ames Cook**

Cold-cathode rings around column feet, guarded by frosted Plexiglas, remain on constantly to satisfy emergency-egress requirements.

Information

project
Le Bonheur Children's Medical Center Memphis, TN
lighting
Craig Roeder
architect
J. Wise Smith Associates, Howard K. Smith Associates
interior
Judy Hall
photographer
Robt. Ames Cook

Like a crayon line, neon sketches the eccentric information desk. The collage of shapes and colors offers a measure of healing relief.

project
Health Central
Orlando, FL
lighting
Craig Roeder
architect
HKS Inc., Architects
interior
HKS Designcare / Mitchell
photographer
Michael Lowry

[left]   Purple neon and 150 PAR38
mercury spots, coupled with dichroic blue
color filters, create palm-leaf patterns.

[below left]   The lighting design
for this nurses station uses a 3200 degrees
Kelvin cold cathode to show off the
architectural detail of a domed ceiling.

project   **California Pacific Medical Center**
            San Francisco, CA
lighting   **Becca Foster Lighting Design**
architect   **Agnes Bourne Inc.**
interior   **Victoria Stone**
photographer **John Vaughan**

This hospital wanted to create a non-denominational meditation chapel
within an existing 15-foot circular space. The small space has furniture
and lighting that are flexible enough for private meditation and for
occasional gatherings of 10 to 12 people. Existing cove lighting was
re-lamped with energy-efficient incandescent lamps. A dimmer increases
lamp longevity and lighting adaptability within the multi-purpose space.
Some of the existing recessed downlights were re-trimmed and re-lamped
to softly wash the faux-marbled surfaces with light.

project   **Milwaukee Heart and Vascular**
              Milwaukee, WI
lighting   **Steven L. Klein, Principal;**
              Lana M. Nathe
architect   **The Cerreta Group**
interior   **Marlene King**
photographer   **Mark F. Heffron**

The lobby's design centers around a luminous murano glass partition wall that separates the lobby from an inside corridor. Faux-daylight effects mimic the character of natural fenestration, without revealing any of the light sources. An unobstructed, continuous interior, wall-washed by two compact metal-halide floods, provides an even, reflective surface. Wall sconces with halogen sources bounce light off of an angled ceiling.

EXTERIOR ENVIRONMENTS

dazzle in the darkness

Good exterior lighting is subtle. It highlights plantings, sculpture, and architecture, without drawing attention to itself. It creates a sense of height and depth, and, most importantly, positive visual impact.

In commercial applications, effective exterior lighting is vital, since profits depend on whether clients, customers, or patrons find their way to places of business. In fact, good lighting

design may be the deciding factor in the success of a business, especially in high-profile endeavors, such as restaurants or nightclubs, where exterior lighting can create the exotic atmosphere that helps an establishment become the popular place to be, instead of just another night spot. And without proper lighting, even the most beautifully designed facade or sign loses its impact at night. Good

exterior lighting can transform a business or public space into a visual landmark that stands out in the crowd.

It's also important to understand that the lighting actually draws people to an entrance. Passersby are drawn to the brightest source of illumination simply by natural tendency. Successful exterior lighting designs exploit this tendency.

In landscaping, lighting design has generally been

overlooked. Huge floodlights and super-bright pole or post lights may provide a lot of illumination, but they do nothing for exterior ambiance. What people end up seeing is a lot of bright glaring lights, and hardly notice the beautiful landscaping or architectural features. Here you will find design techniques and approaches that do their best to capture a piece of the evening sky.

project
**Art Wave '91
Nagoya, Japan**
lighting
**TL Yamagiwa Laboratory,
Nobuyoshi Sakai**
photographer
Yamagiwa Corporation

This sculpture's thousand glowing fiber-optic strands mimic the glow of fireflies.

project	**Morning Park Chikara-Machi**
	Nagoya, Japan
lighting	**Kajima Corporation**
	& Kaplan McLaughlin Diaz
architect	**Kajima Corporation**
	& Kaplan McLaughlin Diaz
photographer	**Yamagiwa Corporation**

When evening comes, neighbors come around to this beautiful courtyard for a walk or have a chat with friends. The courtyard is enhanced by the soft glow of the lighting for the waterfall, pond, trees, and corridor to ensure the comfort of the residents of this community through the lighting.

Miyazaki Train Station Miyazaki Prefecture Japan

A catalyst for center city development, RTKL's design of Miyazaki Station brings an exuberant, high-tech image to this traditional honeymoon resort on Kyushu Island. Grand in scale but not massive in form, the 9000-square-meter train station comprises three distinct elements: a series of deep-blue towers, a horizontally louvered frame that screens the platform from high winds, and a bright yellow canopy running as a continuous wave along the station's retail promenade. On the interior, undulating forms, tropical colors, and light-colored materials reinforce Miyazaki Station's resort character. The ticket wickets straddle the public concourse to allow continuous circulation between the retail zones at each end of the station.

Using speed and movement as metaphors, RTKL created sail-like exterior lighting fixtures that exploit the theme of travel. During the day, the movement of trains and people flicker through the louvered frame across the facade. At night, dramatic bands of light illuminate this facade, creating a rhythmic palette of light and movement.

Placed along the front edge of a series of blue towers, crescent-shaped vertical lanterns provide a consistent rhythm that contrasts with the movement of the trains. These fixtures have a painted steel frame with both clear and white translucent polycarbonate in fill panels. Fluorescent fixtures are attached to a pulley system allowing them to be lowered for replacement and maintenance, with an access panel in the concrete base of the towers.

The horizontally banded space frame is simply uplit by fixtures extended on bracket arms above the wave canopy. The combination of the perforated aluminum panels and the illuminated space frame produces a "time lapse" appearance. The main entrance, made up of three layers of screens with wavy bands of perforated aluminum panels, is similarly lit. These bands change in appearance depending on the viewing angle. At night, a soft glow emanates from the colored panels of white, yellow, and green.

Through imaginative design and lighting, RTKL has transformed a utilitarian structure into a lively city focal point with popular appeal to commuters, tourists, and residents.

project
Miyazaki Train Station Miyazaki, Japan
lighting
RTKL Associates, Inc.
architect
Michi Yamaguchi
photographer
Steven Hall

Grand in scale but not massive in form, the train station comprises three distinct elements: a series of deep-blue towers, a horizontally louvered frame that screens the platform from high winds, and a bright-yellow canopy running as a continuous wave along the station's retail promenade.

project
**Miyazaki Train Station
Miyazaki, Japan**
lighting
RTKL Associates, Inc.
architect
Michi Yamaguchi
photographer
Steven Hall

The close-up of the tower shows its delicately lit form. Custom designed tower fixtures give the structure depth and excitement.

project **Editel**
Boston, MA
lighting **Linda Kondo,**
Clifford Selbert
photographer **Anton Grassl**

This close-up shows the interrelation of
bold lines and vibrant red dots projected
with light.

project **Excalibur**
Las Vegas, NV
lighting **John Renton Young**
architect **Veldon Simpson**
interior **Marnell Carrao**
photographer **Dave Chawla**

Before its transformation, this "castle" had impressive dimensions, but
appeared flat: the wash of illumination produced by the original floodlighting
gave the building no depth. The current lighting design includes layers of light
that highlight each of the castle's unique architectural features. A combination
of focal lighting, floodlighting, and colored lamps creates a make-believe,
ethereal mood and enhances the dimensions of the towers.

project
**Editel
Boston, MA**
lighting
**Linda Kondo,
Clifford Selbert**
photographer
Anton Grassl

Saturated colors from a light sculpture
turns a building to art.

exterior
environments

project
**Westhills Towne Centre
Alberta, Canada**
lighting
**Stebnicki Robertson
and Associates Ltd.**
architect
RTKL Associates Inc.
interior
**Wensley Spotowski
Architectural Group**
photographer
David Whitcomb

Westhills Towne Centre is a single-level neighborhood retail center. The playful building patterns imitate branding-iron and tooled-leather motifs. A monumental pylon evokes regional grain silos. The lighting is designed to let these shapes predominate while calling attention to the setting.

project	**Casino Magic at Biloxi Biloxi, MS**
lighting	**Patrick Gallegos, Principal; Karl Haas**
architect	**Lund & Associates**
interior	**Spectra F/X**
photographer	**Patrick Gallegos**

[below]   This simple design approach creates a flexible and dramatic expression by combining existing technology with cutting-edge fixtures. The porte-cochère translucent fabric is underlit with 650-watt halogen lamps covered with dichroic color filters. Two independently controlled colors provide full-color changes, as well as sweeping variations across the translucent canopy. The lighting by reflection also provides the primary light for under the porte-cochère at the casino entry. Additional halogen floods produce focal accents for the escalator entry paths to the casino. Metal halide downlights create functional lighting for an automobile drop-off.

exterior
environments

project **Anzu, Dallas, TX**
lighting **Paul Draper & Associates**
architect **Paul Draper & Associates**
interior **Paul Draper & Associates**
photographer **Klein & Wilson**

The gray slate wall was designed to draw attention to the entrance and give the visitor a sense of transition from the outer-western world into the restaurant's new and modern Japanese environment. The entry is set back from the street and required establishing presence. The three-foot tall, halo-lit individual letters have a gilded finish and virtually glow with ambient lighting. Up- and down-lighting enhances the rust-colored slate outlining the wall entry's pierced opening. Surrounding lighting helps establish a warm, friendly environment.

Lighting Q and A

Answers to Frequently Asked Questions

As a lighting consultant and lecturer with many years

of experience, I find that the homeowners, architects,

interior designers, and landscape architects with whom

I work often raise similar questions. Some of their

concerns relate to basics about lighting design. Other

questions come up because more and more new

products constantly are appearing on the market, and

consumers can easily become confused while trying

to keep abreast of the latest technology. The field is

indeed changing rapidly, and learning about lighting

is an ongoing process.

What are the main things to consider when selecting lighting for residential use?
First, assess the amount of light needed for a given space. This is determined by functional needs, the height and slope of the ceiling, the color of the room's surfaces, the location of windows and skylights, and the direction the house faces. Second, consider the proper lamps (bulbs) to use for good color rendering of the various surfaces in the space. Try to keep the color temperature of the lamps between 3,000 and 4,000 degrees Kelvin, no matter what source. You can mix incandescent, halogen, fluorescent, low-voltage, and line-voltage sources, as long as their color temperatures are similar.

What are the recommended mounting heights for wall sconces and ceiling fixtures?
Wall sconces normally are mounted at 6 feet (1.8 meters) on 8-foot (2.4-meter) walls and at 6.6 feet (2 meters) on walls that are 9 feet (2.7 meters) or taller. A pendant-hung fixture normally is mounted 36 inches (91 centimeters) above the table or countertop.

Should I install track or recessed lighting?
Track lighting works best when used as accent lighting to highlight paintings and specific objects, and it's a particularly good option when there is not enough ceiling depth for recessed lighting, or in rental units where cost and portability are important. Track lighting does not, however, provide adequate ambient light to warm and soften a room. It is also a poor choice for task lighting because you end up working in your own shadow.

Over the past several years, recessed lighting has greatly improved. Most manufacturers now offer recessed adjustable fixtures that use low-voltage lamps (lamp is the lighting industry's term for a light bulb) and integral transformers. These fixtures offer the clean look of a recessed system with the flexibility of track, and a wide variety of beam spreads can be produced simply by changing the lamp. The big news, however, is that now many of these fixtures are made specifically for remodeling, which makes installation into existing ceilings clean and easy.

What is the best way to avoid glare when lighting artwork on a wall?

Accent light fixtures, such as recessed adjustable and track, should have louvers and be directed onto art from the side, instead of centered on the painting. Any glass or Plexiglas surface becomes a mirror. If the light comes from the side, then the glare is redirected away from the viewer.

What about the energy efficiency of various lighting options?

Incandescent household bulbs are the least energy-efficient choice. Halogen lamps supply approximately twice the amount of light provided by household bulbs of the same wattage. Fluorescents are three to five times more energy efficient than comparable incandescent household bulbs.

How can I get both the color quality of incandescent light and the energy efficiency of fluorescent?

For years, the only choices in fluorescent lamps were warm-white, which actually looked like a blend of pink and orange, and cool-white, which produced a blue-green light that made people look ghoulish. Today all that has changed, and more than 200 colors of fluorescents are available. In addition, the technology of fluorescent components has improved to include a non-humming, full-range dimming ballast line of fixtures.

Should I consider compact fluorescent lamps (CFLs)?

Yes, particularly since this energy-efficient option now comes in such a variety of color temperatures. In addition, CFLs are available that are inside glass envelopes with standard screw-in bases, so the look of the lamp is comfortably familiar. A 9-watt CFL produces light roughly equivalent to 40 watts of incandescent illumination, while a 13-watt CFL is approximately equal to 75 watts worth of incandescent light.

What is a low-voltage lighting system, and what are its advantages?

Low voltage, according to electrical code, is anything under 50 volts (normal house current, also known as line voltage, operates at 110 to 120 volts). The most commonly used low-voltage systems are 12-volt and 6-volt. A transformer lowers line voltage to low voltage. It can be located inside the fixture (integral) or somewhere nearby (remote). Low voltage can produce more light per watt than line voltage—often at as much as a three-to-one ratio. Although low-voltage systems have a higher initial cost, the advantages in energy efficiency and low maintenance are considerable. Low-voltage lamps come in a variety of wattages and beam spreads; you can pinpoint a

bowl of flowers or light a 6-foot (1.8 meter) painting. Currently the most popular low-voltage lamp is the MR16 (multi-mirror reflector), the same type of lamp used in slide projectors.

What is a halogen bulb?

Halogen, also referred to as tungsten halogen or quartz, is an incandescent source that burns at a whiter color temperature than a standard household bulb. As a result, colors are rendered more truly in a space illuminated by halogen. However, like all incandescent sources, a halogen lamp will become more amber when dimmed. Because a halogen lamp has much greater light output than a standard household bulb of equal wattage, you can use a smaller wattage halogen lamp to give an equal amount of light. Halogen sources come in low and line voltage versions.

Can a halogen bulb be touched?

It's best not to touch the glass envelope of most halogen lamps. The oil on your hand attracts dirt to the glass and can create a point of weakness, causing the bulb to burn out prematurely and possibly explode. If you do happen to touch the lamp, clean it with rubbing alcohol.

Do halogen bulbs last longer?

The average rated life for a halogen lamp is 2,000 to 2,500 hours. This means that at the 2,000- to 2,500-hour mark, half the lamps will be burned out and half will still be working. The key to maximizing halogen lamp life is to make sure the bulbs runs at full capacity (turned up all the way rather than dimmed) at least 20 percent of the time it is used. This has a cleaning effect on the inside of the lamp.

If halogen torchieres direct light upward, how can they provide light suitable for reading?

Halogen torchieres provide excellent ambient lighting for a room. If you have a white or light colored ceiling, they also can provide suitable secondary task illumination for reading. However, this reflected light should be used only for light reading, such as perusing newspapers or magazine. For serious reading of books, the best option is a pharmacy-type lamp that positions the light between your head and the page.

Lighting Q and A

For serious reading, is the equivalent of a 60-watt incandescent bulb bright *enough*?
Light levels are a matter of preference, and the distance a person sits from the light source also is a factor. In general, the incandescent bulb in a pharmacy-type lamp which is situated next to the reader at shoulder height should be between 60 and 75 watts.

What are the guidelines for installing skylights?
Often skylights are installed to supplement or replace electric lighting during the daytime hours. Because clear or bronze skylights project a hard light in the shape of the skylight itself onto the floor, select instead a white opal skylight, which diffuses the daylight. Also, always get an ultraviolet inhibitor. It's a standard option and prevents the premature fading and sun rotting of natural materials.

Skylights usually should not be centered over tables or islands because they interfere with the placement of lighting fixtures. However, if the light well is deep enough, fluorescent strip lights can be mounted between the acrylic panel and the skylight to provide nighttime lighting and to keep the skylight from looking like a black hole in the ceiling.

What about using neon and fiber optics for residential lighting?
Local electrical code should be checked before using neon, since some jurisdictions don't permit it in residential spaces. Humming is another consideration. Neon is fine in rooms that have a fair amount of ambient noise, but in quiet areas the inherent hum can be disturbing unless the transformer is put in a remote location. Also, be careful with color selection, since intense neon hues can shift a room's color scheme.

Fiber optics provide a subtle glow of light for edge details, serving as a decorative source only. The illumination from a fiber-optic fixture will be even as long as the fiber optic is looped back into the light source or illuminated from both ends. Otherwise the lighting will be more intense in one end.

How can one avoid glare on shiny dark countertops and backsplashes from under-cabinet fixtures?
This is a common problem and one that is the toughest to solve. Mirror-like finishes reflect everything. One solution is to install a bottom facia piece that shields the fixture from the countertop. The light reflects off the backsplash onto the work surface. The drawback is that much of the light is caught behind the trim piece and never reaches the work surface. A

second solution is to install miniature recessed, adjustable low-voltage fixtures in the cabinet. Each fixture would take up the space about equal to that of a coffee can. These fixtures should be aimed at 45-degree angles to the work surface and louvered to avoid glare.

What is the purpose of recessed incandescent downlighting and when should it not be used?
Recessed fixtures do not provide the best type of general or ambient illumination. Since no light reaches the ceiling, the upper quadrants of the room fall into darkness. This makes the room seem smaller and creates hard shadows on faces. In California all general illumination in new kitchens and baths must be fluorescent.

Where should under-cabinet fixtures be placed?
Place task lights on a level between a person's head and the work surface, mounted tight to the face of the cabinet. Have the light reflect off the backsplash and onto the countertop. Shielding should extend 1 inch (3 centimeters) deeper than the fixture itself. This produces good, shadow-free task light.

Where should fixtures above cabinets be placed to achieve good indirect lighting?
Mount fixtures flush with the front of the cabinets, to prevent bright spots and to be sure objects don't block the light. Add a wood block to fit the display items to the facia level so that they are not visually cut off at the bottom.

Where can fixtures be placed to light the interior of a glass door cabinet?
Fixtures can be recessed above glass shelves. If they are wooden shelves, fixtures can be mounted horizontally on each shelf; or, if the shelves can be set back slightly, the fixtures can be run vertically on the inside edges of the doors.

In high-end, high-budget jobs, do energy considerations still apply?
Whether it's a high-end or an economy project, energy costs should be carefully considered. No one wants to spend more money on energy than is necessary. Incandescent household bulbs are the least energy-efficient. Quartz supplies approximately twice the amount of light provided by household bulbs of the same wattage. Fluorescents give three to fives times the amount of incandescent household bulbs of the same wattage.

Glossary

Absorption: The amount of light taken in by an object instead of being reflected. Dark-colored and matte surfaces have high degrees of absorption.

Accent Lighting: Illumination directed at a particular object in order to draw attention to it.

Ambient Lighting: The soft indirect illumination that fills the volume of a room and creates an inviting glow. Also referred to as fill light.

Amperage: The amount of electrical current that can run through a conductive source.

Ballast: A device that transforms electrical energy used by fluorescent, mercury vapor, high-pressure sodium, or metal halide lamps so that the proper amount of power is provided to the lamp.

Beam Spread: The diameter of the pattern of light produced by a lamp or lamp and luminaire together.

Bridge System: A two-wire low-voltage cable lighting system.

Cold Cathode: A neon-like electric-discharge light source, often a good option for areas that cannot accommodate fluorescent tubes.

Color Rendering Index (CRI): A scale used to measure how well a lamp illuminates an object's color tones as compared with daylight. Color correction refers to the addition of phosphors to a lamp to create a better CRI.

Diffusion Filter: A glass lens used to widen and soften light output.

Dimming Ballast: A device used with fluorescent lamps to control the light level.

Fiber Optic: An illuminating system composed of a lamp source, fibers, and output optics, used to remotely light an area or object.

Filter: A glass or metal accessory that alters beam patterns.

Fluorescent Lamp: A very energy efficient lamp that produces light by activating the phosphor coating on the inside surface of a glass envelope.

Footcandle: A term used to measure the amount of light hitting a surface.

Framing Projector: A luminaire that can be precisely adjusted to frame an object with light.

Glare or Glare Factor: Uncomfortably bright light that becomes the focus of attention rather than the area or object it was meant to illuminate.

Halogen: An incandescent lamp containing halogen gas that recycles tungsten. Halogen lamps burn hotter and brighter than standard incandescent lamps.

High-Intensity Discharge (HID) Lamp: A type of lamp primarily used in exterior settings that emits bright, energy-efficient light by electrically activating pressurized gas in a bulb. Mercury vapor, metal halide, and high-pressure sodium lamps are all HID sources.

High Pressure Sodium: HID lamp that uses sodium vapor as the light-producing element. It provides a yellow-orange light.

Housing: The above-the-ceiling enclosure for a luminaire's recessed socket and trim.

Incandescent Lamp: The traditional type of light bulb that produces light through electricity causing a filament to glow.

Kelvin: A measure of color temperature.

Kilowatt: A measure of electrical usage. One thousand watts equals one kilowatt.

Lamp: The lighting industry's term for a light bulb, i.e. a glass envelope with a coating, filament, or gas that glows when electricity is applied.

Line Voltage: The 120-volt household current generally standard in North America.

Louver: A meal accessory used on a luminaire to prevent glare.

Low-Pressure Sodium Lamp: A discharge lamp that uses sodium vapor as the light-producing element. It produces an orange-gray light.

Low-Voltage Lighting: A system that uses a current less than 50 volts (commonly 12 volts) instead of the standard household current of 120 volts. A transformer converts the electrical power to the appropriate voltage.

Luminaire: The complete light fixture with all parts and lamps (bulb) necessary for positioning and obtaining power supply.

Mercury Lamp: HID lamps where light emission is radiated mainly from mercury. They can be clear, phosphor-coated, or self-ballasted. They produce a bluish light.

Metal Halide Lamp: HID lamps where light comes from radiation from metal halides. It produces the whitest light of the HID sources.

Mirror Reflecting Lamps (MR11, MR16): Miniature tungsten halogen lamps with a variety of wattages and beam spreads, controlled by mirrors positioned in the reflector.

Neon Light: A glass vacuum tube filled with neon gas and phosphors, frequently formed into signs or letters.

PAR Lamps: Lamps (bulbs) with parabolic aluminized reflectors that give exacting beam control ranging from a wide flood to a very narrow spot. PAR lamps can be used outdoors due to their thick glass, which holds up in severe weather conditions.

R Lamp: An incandescent source with a built-in reflecting surface.

Reflectance: The ratio of light reflected from a surface.

Reflected Ceiling Plan: A lighting plan drawn from the floor looking at the ceiling above.

RLM Reflector: A luminaire designed to reflect light down, preventing upward transmission.

Spread Lens: A glass lens accessory used to diffuse and widen beam patterns.

Task Lighting: Illumination designed for a work surface so that good light, free of shadows and glare, is present.

Transformer: A device that raises or lowers voltage, generally used for low-voltage lights.

Tungsten-Halogen: A tungsten incandescent lamp (bulb) containing gas that burns hotter and brighter than standard incandescent lamps.

Voltage: A measurement of the pressure of electricity going through a wire.

Voltage Drop: A decrease of electrical pressure in low-voltage lighting systems, which occurs as a fixture's distance from the transformer increases, causing a drop in the light output.

White Light: Usually refers to light with a color temperature between 5,000 and 6,250 degrees Kelvin, which is composed of the entire visible light spectrum. This light allows all colors in the spectrum on an object's surface to be reflected, providing good color-rendering qualities. Daylight is the most common source of white light.

Xenon: An inert gas used as a component in certain lamps to produce a cooler color temperature than standard incandescent. Xenon results in a longer lamp life then halogen.

Directory of Architects and Designers

Ace Architects
330 2nd St. Suite 1
Oakland, CA 94607
(510) 452-0775

Pam Ackerman
Design Lighting Resource, Inc.
8361 East Evans, Suite 108
Scotsdale, AZ 85260
(602) 991-5655

Rik Adams
Adams/Mohler Architects
3515 Fremont Ave. N.
Seattle, WA 98103
(206) 632-2443

Eugene Anthony & Associates
2408 Fillmore St.
San Francisco, CA 94115
(415) 567-9575

Architectural Interiors
162 Parliament St.
Toronto, Ontario M5E 221 Canada
(416) 367-9144

Nancy Arriano, ASID
Plunkett Raysich Architects
10850 W. Park Place, Suite 300
Milwaukee, WI 53224
(414) 359-3060

Len Auerbach, ASTC
S. Leonard Auerbach &
Associates, Inc.
1045 Sansome St., #218
San Francisco, CA 94111
(415) 392-7528

Lynn AugStein, ASID, CID
LAS Design
3 Wolfback Terrace
Sausalito, CA 94965
(415) 332-3323

Aumiller Youngquist, P.C.
111 E. Busse Ave., Suite 603
Mt. Prospect, Il 60056
(708) 253-3761

Axiom Design Inc.
56718 Sonoma Dr.
Pleasanton, CA 94566
(510) 462-2300

Babey—Moulton, Inc.
14 Gold St.
San Francisco, CA 94133
(415) 394-9910

Backen Arrigoni and Ross
Architects
1660 Bush St.
San Francisco, CA 94109
(415) 441-4771

Sheron Bailey
Design Ideas
12390 Ave. 8
Chowchilla, CA 93610
(209) 665-4515

Hiram Banks, LIT
Lighting Integration Technology,
Inc.
10 Arkansas St.
San Francisco, CA 94107
(415) 863-0313

Richard Bartlett, AIA
Theatre Square, Suite 217
Orinda, CA 94563
(510) 253-2880

Lou Ann Bauer
Bauer Interior Design
239 Broderick St.
San Francisco, CA 94117
(415) 621-7262

Mike Beam
Reid and Tarics Associates
55 Hawthorne St., Suite 400
San Francisco, CA 94105
(415) 546-7123

David W. Beer
Brennan Beer Gorman/Architects
515 Madison Ave.
New York, NY 10022
(212) 888-7663

Leonor Bedel, IALD
Leonor Bedel & Associates
Avda. Juan De Garay 325 4B7
Buenos Aires, 1153 Argentina
(541) 361-9792

Teri Behm
Behm Architects
1325 Filbert St.
San Francisco, CA 94109
(415) 263-1755

Andrew Belschner
Andrew Belschner Joseph Vincent
821 Sansome St.
San Fransisco, CA 94111
(415) 982-1215

Hamlet C. "Lucky" Bennett
78-6697 A Mam La Hoa Hwy.
Holua Loa, HI 96725
(808) 322-3375

James Benya, PE, FIES
Senior Principal
Luminae Souter Lighting Design
1740 Army St., 2nd Floor
San Francisco, CA 94124
(415) 285-2622

David Birn
Skylight Opera Theatre Artists
158 North Broadway
Milwaukee, WI 53202
(414) 291-7811

Mil Bodron Design
2801 West Lemmon Ave.
Suite 201
Dallas, TX 75204
(214) 871-7588

Cynthia Bolton-Karasik,
Designer
The Lighting Group
200 Pine St. #200
San Francisco, CA 94104
(415) 989-3446

Bill Booziotis
Booziotis & Co.
2400 A Empire Central Dr.
Dallas, TX 75235
(514) 350-5051

Bradley A. Bouch
Spectrum Lighting Design
6767 West Tropicana, #208
Las Vegas, NV 89103
(702) 248-1057

Agnes C. Bourne, ASID
Agnes C. Bourne, Inc.
Two Henry Adams St., Space 220
San Francisco, CA 94103
(415) 626-6883

Barbara Bouyea, IALD, IES
Bouyea & Associates
3811 Turtle Creek Blvd., Suite
1010
Dallas, TX 75219
(214) 520-6580

Teal Brogden
Horton Lees Lighting Design
1011 Kearny St.
San Francisco, CA 94133
(415) 986-2575

George Brook-Kothlow &
Assoicates
P.O. Box AD
Carmel, CA 93921
(408) 659-4596

Sandra Brown Interiors Inc.
537 Sycamore Valley Rd. West
Danville, CA 94526
(510) 837-1370

Kathleen Buoymaster Inc.
6933 La Jolla Blvd.
La Jolla, CA 92037
(619) 456-2850

Gunner Burklund
Grebmeier Burklund
1298 Sacramento St.
San Francisco, CA 94108
(415) 931-1088

Sherrill Bushfield
Raintree Design
15957 Marine Dr.
White Rock, BC V4B 1G1
Canada
(604) 538-2216

Lewis Butler
Butler Armsden Architects
524 2nd St.
San Francisco, CA 94107
(415) 495-5495

Edward J. Cansino and Associates
1620 School St., Suite 102
Moraga, CA 94556
(510) 376-9497

Cardwell/Thomas & Associates,
Inc.
1221 Second Ave., Suite 300
Seattle, WA 98101
(206) 622-2311

Albert Carey, ASID
Acorn Kitchens and Baths
4640 Telegraph Ave.
Oakland, CA 94609
(510) 547-6581

Jeff Carloss
Jordon Mozer & Associates, Ltd.
228 W. Illinois
Chicago, IL 60610
(312) 661-0060

Carla Carstens' Designs
1 Timber View Rd.
Soquel, CA 95073
(408) 462-4775

Jere Cavanaugh
Rio Volga 17-6
DF 06500 Mexico
011-525-514-7529

Diane Chapman Interiors
3380 Washington St.
San Francisco, CA 94118
(415) 346-2373

Sidney C. L. Char
Wimberly Allison Tong & Goo
2222 Kalakana Ave.
Honolulu, HI 96815
(808) 922-1253

Peggy Chestnut Interior Design
c/o Maryl Development
75-174 Kuakini Highway
Suite 101A
Kailua-Kona, HI 96740
(808) 329-9370

Clanton Engineering
4699 Nautilus Court South, Suite 101
Boulder, CO 80301
(303) 530-7229

Debbie Collins, ASID
Ruth Soforenko & Associates
137 Forest Ave.
Palo Alto, CA 94301
(415) 326-5448

James Connelly Interiors
5621 North Lake Dr.
Milwaukee, WI 53217
(414) 332-0610

Gene Conti, AIA
Richard Pollack & Associates
214 Grant Ave., Suite 450
San Francisco, CA 94108
(415) 788-4400

Bernard Corday Lighting Design
615 Parrott Dr.
San Manteo, CA 94402
(415) 340-9175

Marcia Cox, ASID
Marcia Cox Interiors
133 Stone Pine Lane
Menlo Park, CA 94025
(415) 322-4307

CRSS Architects, Inc.
444 South Flower St., 4th Floor
Los Angeles, CA 90071
(213) 688-3097

Ian Curry
Cathedral Architect's Office
The Great Kitchen, The College
Durham, DHI 3EQ
United Kingdom
44-0171-384-7010

Dahlin Group
2671 Crow Canyon Dr.
San Ramone, CA 94583
(510) 837-8286

Richard D'Amico
D'Amico and Partners Inc.
1402 First Ave. S.
Minneapolis, MN 55403
(612) 334-3366

Ross De Alessi, IALD, MIES
Ross De Alessi Lighting Design
4370 Alpine Rd. Suite 210
Portola Valley, CA 94028
(415) 854-6924

Winifred Dell'Ario
Design Dell'Ario
P.O. Box 3266
Half Moon Bay, CA 94109
(415) 726-7122

Michael DiBlasi, USITT
Schuler & Shook, Inc.
123 Third St. N., Suite 216
Minneapolis, MN 55401
(612) 339-5958

Peter Dominick, FAIA
Urban Design Group
1621 18th St., Suite 200
Denver, CO 80202
(303) 292-3388

Richard Drummond Davis
4310 Westside Dr., Suite H
Dallas, TX 75209
(214) 521-8763

Roger C. Duffala
DVT Design Group
1200 West Platt St.
Suite 201
Tampa, FL 33606
(813) 253-6068

David Ebert
Horton Lees Lighting Design
1011 Kearny St.
San Francisco, CA 94133
(415) 986-2575

Ehrlich Rominger Architects
4800 El Camino Real
Los Altos, CA 94022
(415) 949-1300

Einhorn Yaffee Prescott
The Argus Bldg. Broadway at Beaver
P.O. Box 617
Albany, NY 12201-0617
(518) 431-3420

Wallace G. Eley, IES, PEO
Crossey Engineering Ltd.
4141 Yonge St., Suite 305
Toronto, Ontario M2P 2A8
Canada
(416) 221-3111

ELS/Elbasani & Logan Architects
2040 Addison Court
Berkeley, CA 94704
(510) 549-2929

Fumio Enomoto
Enomoto Atelier
2-28-31 Chuo, Nakano-ku
Tokyo, 164 Japan
81-3-5330-5696

Joe Esherick
EHDD
2789 25th St., 3rd Floor
San Francisco, CA 94110
(415) 285-9193

Linda Esselstein, MIES
1495 Altschul Ave.
Menlo Park, CA 94025
(415) 854-6924

Estudio Arthur de Mattos
Casas Ltda
Alameda Ministro Rocha
Azevedo, 1052
Sao Paulo, Sao Paulo
01410-002 Brazil
011-55-11-282-6311

Cheri Etchelecu Interior Design
9400 North Central Expressway, #1605
Dallas, TX 75231-5045
(214) 369-7486

Linda Ferry IESNA, ASID (affiliate)
Architectural Illumination
P.O. Box 2690
Monterey, CA 93942
(408) 649-3711

Stan Field
3631 Evergreen Dr.
Palo Alto, CA 94303
(415) 462-9554

Toby Flax Interior Design Studio
444 DeHaro St., #122
San Francisco, CA 94107
(415) 252-8184

Fleischman/Garcia Architects
324 Hyde Park Ave., Suite 300
Tampa, FL 33606
(813) 251-4400

Dan Fletcher
Fletcher + Hardoin
769 Pacific St.
Monterey, CA 93940
(408) 373-5855

Forrest Architects
525 Broadway
Sonoma, CA 95476
(707) 935-1570

C.H. Ned Forrest
Forrest Architects
525 Broadway
Sonoma, CA 95476
(707) 935-1570

Becca Foster Lighting Design
27 South Park
San Francisco, CA 94107
(415) 541-0370

Gary Francis & Associates
P.O. Box 2129
Park City, UT 84060
(801) 649-7168

Janet Gay Freed
Janet Freed Interior Design
295 South St.
Sausalito, CA 94965
(415) 332-2572

Larry French, IALD, IES, USITT
S. Leonard Auerbach & Associates, Inc.
1045 Sansome St.
San Francisco, CA 94111
(415) 392-7528

Frank Frost
Frost/Tsuchi Architects
915 Battery St.
San Francisco, CA 94111
(415) 421-9339

Patrick Gallegos
Gallegos Lighting Design
8132 Andasol Ave.
Northridge, CA 91325
(818) 343-5762

Gandy/Peace, Inc.
3195 Paces Ferry Place N.W.
Atlanta, GA 30305-1307
(404) 237-8681

David Gast and Associates
1746 Union St.
San Francisco, CA 94123
(415) 885-2946

Steve Geiszler
Rupel, Geiszler McLedd
522 Brannan St.
San Francisco, CA 94107
(415) 243-9440

Gensler & Associates
600 California St.
San Francisco, CA 94108
(415) 627-3563

Sarah J. Gibson, IESNA, IALD
Archillume Lighting Design
3701 Executive Center Dr., #150
Austin, TX 78731
(512) 346-1386

James Gillam Architects
1841 Powell St.
San Francisco, CA 94133
(415) 398-1120

Patricia Glasow, IALD
S. Leonard Auerbach & Associates, Inc.
1045 Sansome St., #218
San Francisco, CA 94111
(415) 392-7528

Sharad Gokarna
Brennan Beer Gorman Monk/ Interiors
515 Madison Ave.
New York, NY 10022
(212) 888-7663

Peter Gorman, AIA
Brennan Beer Gorman Monk/Architects
515 Madison Ave.
New York, NY 10022
(212) 888-7663

Stefan Graf, IALD, IES
Illuminart
404 North River
Ypsilanti, MI 48198
(313) 482-6066

Charles J. Grebmeier, ASID
Grebmeier-Roy Design
1298 Sacramento St.
San Francisco, CA 94108
(415) 931-1088

Marty Greg
Weber Design, Inc.
1439 Larimer Square
Denver, CO 80202
(303) 892-9816

Russell Greey
Brant & Greey
1110 East Missouri
Phoenix, AZ 85014
(602) 222-8848

Charles Paxton Gremillion
Loyd-Paxton Inc.
3636 Maple Ave.
Dallas, TX 75219
(214) 521-1521

Courtney Griffith Interiors
300 Summit Dr.
Corte Madera, CA 94925
(415) 924-5699

Karl Haas
Gallegos Lighting Design
8132 Andasol Ave.
Northridge, CA 91325
(818) 343-5762

Barbara Haigh
Haigh . Architects . Designers
125 Greenwich Ave.
Greenwich, CT 06830
(203) 869-5445

Paul Haigh, AIA
Haigh . Architects . Designers
125 Greenwich Ave.
Greenwich, CT 06830
(203) 869-5445

David Hale, AIA
256 Sutter St., #500
San Francisco, CA 94108
(415) 982-1216

Holly Hall
Booziotis & Co.
2400 A Empire Central Dr.
Dallas, TX 75235
(214) 350-5051

Jessica Hall Associates
1301 6th St., Suite G
San Francisco, CA 94107-2222
(415) 552-9923

Judy Hall c/o Le Bonheur Hospital
50 N. Dunlap St.
Memphis, TN 38103
(901) 572-3000

Naokazu Hanadoh
Shimizu Corporation
Seabanse S., 1-2-3 Shibaura,
Minato-ku
Tokyo, 105-07
Japan
81-3-5441-0222

Richard Hannum, AIA
Hannum Associates
222 Sutter St., Suite 400
San Francisco, CA 94108
(415) 543-8333

Phil Hardoin
Flectcher + Hardoin
769 Pacific St.
Monterey, CA 93940
(408) 373-5855

Michael Helm
200 7th Ave., #110
Santa Cruz, CA 95062
(408) 476-5386

Jerry Hettinger
J. Hettinger Interiors
200 Hartz Ave.
Danville, CA 94526
(510) 820-9336

Hirsh Bedner Associates
3216 Nebraska Ave.
Santa Monica, CA 90404
(310) 829-9087

HKS Architects
700 N. Pearl, Suite 1100, LB 307
Dallas, TX 75201
(214) 969-5599

HOK Inc.
71 Stevenson St., Suite 2200
San Francisco, CA 94105
(415) 2443-0555

Stephen D. Holzhaver, AIA
Plunkett Raysich Architects
10850 W. Park Place
Suite 300
Milwaukee, WI 53224
(414) 359-3060

Michael Hopkins, CBE, RA,
AADip, RIBA
Michael Hopkins and Partners
27 Broadley Terrace
London, NW1 6LG England
0171-724-1751

Patty Hopkins, AADip
Michael Hopkins and Partners
27 Broadley Terrace
London, NW1 6LG England
0171-724-1751

Mark R. Hornberger, AIA
Hornberger + Worstell
170 Maiden Lane, Suite 170
San Francisco, CA 94108
(415) 391-1080

Horton Lees Lighting Design
1011 Kearny St.
San Francisco, CA 94133
(415) 986-2575

Susan Huey
Lighting Intergration Technology,
Inc.
10 Arkansas St., Suite C
San Francisco, CA 94107
(415) 863-0313

Huntsman Associates
465 California Street, #1000
San Francisco, CA 94104
(415) 394-1212

Janis Huston, IES, IALD
Sand Dollar—A Lighting Design
Co.
932 Tsawwassen Beach
South Delta, BC V4M 2J3
Canada
(604) 943-5641

Ikuei Ikeda
Yoshimura Architects &
Associates, Inc.
28 Kamimiyanomae-cho,
Sishigatani, Sakyo-ku
Kyoto, 606 Japan
075-771-6071

Interior Architects
350 California St., Suite 1500
San Francisco, CA 94104
(415) 434-3305

Chip Israel, IALD, IES
Lighting Design Alliance
1234 East Burnett St.
Long Beach, CA 90806-3510
(310) 989-3843

Barbara Jacobs Interior Design
12340 Saratoga-Sunnyvale Rd.
Saratoga, CA 95070
(408) 446-2225

Duane Johnson, IESNA
Artistic Lighting Corp.
767 Lincoln Ave., Suite 8
San Rafael, CA 94901
(415) 456-1656

J. B. Johnson Arquiteto
Rio Volga 17-6
DF 06500 Mexico
011-525-514-7529

Steve Johnson
Roeder-Johnson Corp.
655 Skyway, Suite 130
San Carlos, CA 94074
(415) 802-1852

Kajima Corporation
6-5-30 Akasaka, Minato-ku
Tokyo, 107 Japan
81-3-5661-2244

Joe Kaplan Lighting Design
9023 Hopen Place
Los Angeles, CA 90069
(310) 652-4795

Kaplan McLaughlin Diaz
222 Vallejo St.
San Francisco, CA 94111
(415) 398-5191

Cynthia Bolton Karasik
The Lighting Group
200 Pine St.
San Francisco, CA 94109
(415) 989-3446

Hiroshi Kawaguchi
Yoshimura Architect & Associates,
Inc.
28 Kamimiyanomae-cho,
Shishigatani
Sakyo-ku
Kyoto 606 Japan
075-771-6071

Frank Kelly
Imero Fiorentino Associates
33 West 60th St.
New York, NY 10019
(212) 246-0600

Marlene King
864 Honey Creek Parkway
Wauwatosa, WI 53214
(414) 475-6879

Kenji Kitani
Kitani Design Associates, Inc.
City Pole 4-5, 4-Chome,
Awatimachi Chuo-ku
Osaka, 541 Japan
06-232-1641

Kennedy Lutz Architecture
764 P St., Suite B
Fresno, CA 93721
(209) 497-8035

Allen Kirsch Interior Design
3131 Turtle Creek, Suite 820
Dallas, TX 75219
(214) 526-5496

Steven L. Klein
Standard Electric Supply Co.
222 North Emmber Lane
Milwaukee, WI 53233
(800) 776-8222

Kenton Knapp, ASID
Kenton Knapp Design
P.O. Box 2498
Santa Cruz, CA 95063
(408) 476-7547

Linda Kondo
Clifford Selbert Design
Collaborative
2067 Massachusetts Ave.
Cambridge, MA 02140
(617) 497-6605

Yasuo Kondo
Yasuo Kondo Design Office
Bond St. T-3 2F
2-2-43 Higashi Shinagawa,
Shinagawa-ku
Tokyo, 140 Japan
81-3-3458-1185

Theo Kondos, IALD
Theo Kondos Associates
13 West 36th St.
New York, NY 10018
(212) 736-5510

Anna Kondolf Lighting Design
94 Toyon Dr.
Fairfax, CA 94930
(415) 456-5472

Kazubiko Kurako
Shimizu Corporation
Seabanse S., 1-2-3 Shibaura,
Minato-ku
Tokyo, 105-07 Japan
81-3-5441-0222

William C. Lam
Lam Partners Inc.
84 Sherman St.
Cambridge, MA 02140
(617) 354-4502

Bobbie Dawn Lander
3602 Beltline Rd.
Sunnyvale, TX 75182
(972) 226-2701

Todd B. Lankenau
Lundahl and Associates
1755 E. Plumb Lane, Suite 218
Reno, NV 89502
(702) 348-7777

Lorraine Lazowick, ASID
5132 Redbud Grove Lane
Roseville, CA 95747
(916) 771-4601

Sid Del Mar Leach, ASID
Classic Design Associates
288 Butterfield Rd.
San Anselmo, CA 94960
(415) 454-3733

Craig Leavitt, ASID
Leavitt/Weaver, Inc.
451 Tully Rd.
Modesto, CA 95350
(209) 521-5125

Jim Leggit
RNL Design
1225 17th St., Suite 1700
Denver, CO 80202
(303) 295-1717

Allan Leibow, IALD
Wheel Gersztoff Shankar
Lighting Designers
5855 Green Valley Circle
Suite 304
Culver City, CA 90230
(310) 216-1670

Hal LeJeune
Aesthetic Lighting
701 Welch Rd., #323
Palo Alto, CA 94304
(415) 328-3440

Claudia Librett
Design Studio Inc.
311 East 72nd St.,
Penthouse C
New York, NY 10021
(212) 772-0521

Lighting Design Partnership Ltd.
4 John's Place
Edinburgh, EH6 7EL Scotland
44-0-131-553-6633

Alan Lindsley
Lindsley-McCoy Architecture &
Lighting
221 Main St., Suite 940
San Francisco, CA 94105

Vasco Andrade Lopes
Luiz Fernando Rocco
Arquitetos Associados S/C
Rua Mandari, 465-A
Sao Paulo, Sao Paulo
01457-020 Brazil
011-55-11-814-6963

Robert R. Lowe, AIA, AIJ
Stom Ushidate + Interspace Time
Dai-ni Orient Building
5-13-11 Ueno Taito-ku
Tokyo, 110 Japan
03-3836-7293

David Ludwig
Jared Polsky and Associates
469-B Magnolia Ave.
Larkspur, CA 94939
(415) 927-1156

Richard Luke Architects
2605 South Decatur Blvd.
Las Vegas, NV 89102
(702) 876-2520

John G.H. Lum
John G.H. Lum Architect
165 Downey St.
San Francisco, CA 94117
(415) 753-1136

Lund & Associates
1542 E. Beach Blvd.
Gulfport, MS 39501
(601) 863-8700

Jeffrey A. Lundahl
Lundahl and Associates
1755 E. Plumb Lane, Suite 218
Reno, NV 89502
(702) 348-7777

Rhonda Luongo, ASID, CCID
Devlyn Corp.
205 Crystal Springs Center,
Suite 104
San Mateo, CA 94402
(415) 579-2594

Valera W. Lyles
P.O. BOX 223513
Carmel, CA 93922

Maki and Associates
3-6-2 Nihonbashi, Chuoh-ku
Tokyo, 103 Japan
03-3274-6681

David Malman
Architectural Lighting Design
370 Brannan St.
San Francisco, CA 94107
(415) 495-4085

William Manly Associates, Inc.
301 North Water St.
Milwaukee, WI 53201
(414) 291-5200

Paul Marantz, IALD
Fisher Marantz Renfro Stone
126 Fifth Ave.
New York, NY 10011
(212) 691-3020

Brendt Markee
744 N 35th St.
Seattle, WA 98103
(206) 634-1270

William David Martin &
Associates
P.O. Box 2053
Monterey, CA 93940
(408) 373-7101

Ron Martino, ASID
Martino's Interiors
111 N. Santa Cruz Ave.
Los Gatos, CA 95030
(408) 354-9111

James Marzo
James Marzo Design
251 Rhode Island St., Suite 211
San Francisco, CA 94103
(415) 626-7250

Lawrence Masnada Design
1745 20th St.
San Francisco, CA 94107
(415) 641-8364

Koucaku Matsumoto, ICI
Kitani Design Associates
City Pole 4 5, 4 Chome
Awajimachi, Chuo-ku
Osaka, Osaka 541
Japan
011-81-06-232-1641

Anne Maurice
1456 Jefferson St.
San Francisco, CA 9412
(415) 885-4022

Donald Maxcy, ASID
Maxcy Design
Lincoln between 7th & 8th
P.O. Box 5507
Carmel, CA 93921
(408) 625-5081

Patricia Borba McDonald
McDonald & Moore Ltd.
20 N. Almaden Ave.
San Jose, CA 95110
(408) 292-6997

Ann McKenzie
Habitat, Inc.
6031 South Maple Ave.
Tempe, AZ 85283
(602) 345-8442

Kauro Mende
Lighting Planners Associates, Inc.
2-9-3 Minami Aoyama, Minato-ku
Tokyo, 107 Japan
81-3-3796-1811

Joszi Meskan
Joszi Meskan Associates
479 Ninth St.
San Francisco, CA 94010
(415) 431-0500

Tina Messner
4418 Smoke Tree Lane
Concord, CA 94521
(510) 682-9656

Frederick Miley Designs
345 Vermont
San Francisco, CA 94103
(415) 931-5605

Miller Hanson Westerbeck Berger,
Inc.
1201 Hawthorne Ave.
Minneapolis, MN 55403
(612) 332-5420

Bob Miller
Flegels
870 Santa Cruz Ave.
Menlo Park, CA 94025
(415) 326-9661

Jeff Miller
Bent Severin & Associates
(formerly Lightsource, Inc.)
1927 Post Alley
Seattle, WA 98101
(206) 728-5665

Naomi Miller, IALD, IESNA
Lighting Research Center
School of Architecture
Rensselaer Polytechnic Institute
Troy Street
New York, NY 12180-3590
(518) 276-8718

Mitsubishi Estate Co., Ltd.
2-4-1 Marunouchi, Chiyoda-Ku
Tokyo, Japan
813-3502-4672

Rick Mohler
Adams/Mohler Architects
3515 Fremont Ave. N.
Seattle, WA 98103
(206) 632-2443

Julia F. Monk, AIA, ASID
Brennan Beer Gorman
Monk/Interiors
515 Madison Ave.
New York, NY 10022
(212) 888-7663

Ahnalisa Moore Design
280 Grove Acre
Pacific Grove, CA 93950
(408) 649-3925

Marcia Moore
McDonald & Moore Ltd.
20 N. Almaden Ave.
San Jose, CA 95110
(408) 292-6997

Hideto Mori
Lighting Planners Associates, Inc.
2-9-3 Minami Aoyama, Minato-ku
Tokyo, 107 Japan
81-3-3796-1811

Pam Morris Designs
Exciting Lighting
14 E. Sir Francis Blvd.
Larkspur, CA 94939
(415) 925-0840

Kazuhiro Motomachi
Tohata Architect & Associates
4-4-10 Fushimi-Cho, Chuo-ku
Osaka Japan
81-06-202-0391

Janey Lennox Moyer, IALD, IES, ASID
6225 Chelton Dr.
Oakland, CA 94611-2430
(510) 482-9193

Jordan Mozer
Jordan Mozer & Associates, Ltd.
228 W. Illinois
Chicago, IL 60610
(312) 661-0060

G.K. Muennig
G.K. Muennig Architect
P.O. Box 92
Big Sur, CA 93920
(408) 667- 2471

Lana Nathe, IES
Standard Electric Supply Co.
222 N. Emmber Lane
Milwaukee, WI 53233
1-800-776-8222 / (414) 272-8100

John Newcomb
P.O. Box 671
Carmel, CA 93921
(408) 624-9637

Catherine Ng, IES
Vice Principal
Light Source Design Group
1246 18th St.
San Francisco, CA 94107
(415) 626-1210

Anthony Ngai, AIA
A. K. Ngai & Associates
11678 Laurelcrest Dr.
Studio City, CA 91604
(818) 763-5567

Alan Ohashi
Ohashi Design Studio
5739 Presley Ave.
Berkeley, CA 94618
(510) 652-8840

Joy Ohashi
Ohashi Design Studio
5739 Presley Ave.
Berkeley, CA 94618
(510) 652-8840

Terry Ohm
Ohm Productions
601 Minnesota St.
San Francisco, CA 94107
(415) 641-1161

Rolf Olhausen, AIA
Prentice & Chan, Ohlhausen
Architects
14 E. 4th St.
New York, NY 10012
(212) 420-8600

Yukio Oka
Rise Lighting Design Office
1-10-16-903 Minami Senba,
Chuo-ku
Osaka, 542 Japan
06-266-3773

Joan Malter Osburn, ASID
Osburn Design
200 Kansas St., Suite 208
San Francisco, CA 94103
(415) 487-2333

Steven Osburn, ASID
Osburn Design
3315 Sacramento St.
Suite 510
San Francisco, CA 94118
(415) 386-2589

Robert Osten, Jr.
Lam Partners Inc.
84 Sherman St.
Cambridge, MA 02140
(617) 354-4502

Takae Oyake, IALD, IESNA, ASID
Lumenworks
1121 Ranleigh Way, Suite 100
Piedmont, CA 94610
(510) 835-7600

Guinter Parschalk
RDX-Radix Comercial Ltda
Rua Fernando Falcao, 121
Sao Paulo, Sao Paulo
03180-001 Brazil
011-5-11-291-0944

Suzanne Parsons
Parsons Design Group
251 Post St., Suite 412
San Francisco, CA 94104
(415) 981-0990

Albert Pastine Architect
1183 Shotwell
San Francisco, CA
(415) 826-9292

David W. Patton, IES
Intelectric
3333 Kimberly Way
San Mateo, CA 94403
(415) 574-2371

Bill Pearson
Fee Munson Ebert
500 Montgomery St.
San Francisco, CA 94111
(415) 434-0320

Pamela Pennington, ASID, IBD
Pamela Pennington Studios
508 Waverley St.
Palo Alto, CA 94301
(415) 328-1767

Richard Perlstein, AIA
Jared Polsky and Associates
469-B Magnolia Ave.
Larkspur, CA 94939
(415) 927-1156

Dan Phipps & Associates
1031 Post St.
San Francisco, CA 94109
(415) 776-1606

Graham Phoenix, IALD
Lighting Design
63 Gee St.
London, ECIV 3RS United
Kingdom
0171-250-3200

Cosimo Pizzulli
Pizzulli Associates, Inc.
718 Wilshire Blvd.
Santa Monica, CA 90401-1708
(310) 393-9572

Jared Polsky and Associates
469-B Magnolia Ave.
Larkspur, CA 94939
(415) 927-1156

Joe Prados
Laurie Smith Design Associates
407 B East 6th St., #204
Austin, TX 78701
(512) 477-7683

Helen C. Reuter
Details, Inc.
1250 Jones St., #1102
San Francisco, CA 94109
(415) 921-3236

RIA (Reseach Institure of Architecture)
2-12-26 Kohnan Minato-ku
Tokyo, 108 Japan
03-3458-0611

Marilyn Riding Design
12340 Saratoga-Sunnyvale Rd.
Suite 2-3
Saratoga, CA 95070
(408) 446-3166

David Robinson, AIA
Robinson, Mills + Williams
160 Pine St.
San Francisco, CA 94111
(415) 781-9800

Robinson, Mills + Williams
160 Pine St.
San Francisco, CA 94111
(415) 781-9800

Luiz Fernando Rocco
Luiz Fernando Rocco
Arquitetos Associados S/C
Rua Mandari, 465-A
Sao Paulo, Sao Paulo
01457-020 Brazil
011-55-11-814-6963

Craig A. Roeder & Associates
3829 North Hall St.
Dallas, TX 75219
(214) 528-2300

Nan Rosenblatt, Allied Member ASID
Nan Rosenblatt Interior Design
310 Townsend St.
Suite 200
San Francisco, CA 94107
(415) 495-0444

Craig A. Roeder & Associates
3829 North Hall St.
Dallas, TX 75219
(214) 528-2300

Gregory Rothweiler
Shea Architects
100 N Sixth St., Suite 300
Minneapolis, MN 55403
(612) 339-2257

Mark Rudiger
S. Leonard Auerbach & Associates, Inc.
1045 Sansome, #218
San Francisco, CA 94111
(415) 392-7528

Joseph Ruggiero & Associates
4512 Louise Ave.
Encino, CA 91316
(818) 783-9257

Ken Rupel
Rupel, Geiszler McLedd
522 Brannan St.
San Francisco, CA 94107
(415) 243-9440

Nobuyoshi Sakai
4-22-2 Kagamiike, Chikusaku
Nagoya-shi
Ehime Japan

Priscilla Sanchez Interiors
444 De Haro St., Suite 101
San Francisco, CA 94107
(415) 864-7766

Mary Ann Schicketanz
Carver & Schicketanz
P.O. Box 2684
Carmel, CA 93921
(408) 624-2304

John Schneider Design
P.O. Box 1457
Pebble Beach, CA 93953
(408) 649-8221

Rick Schreiber, FARA, IBD
Habitat, Inc.
6031 South Maple Ave.
Tempe, AZ 85283
(602) 345-8442

Duane Schuler, IALD, IES
Schuler & Shook, Inc.
123 3rd St. N., Suite 216
Minneapolis, MN 56401
(612) 339-5958

Candra Scott
Candra Scott & Associates
30 Langton St.
San Francisco, CA 94103
(415) 861-0690

Sherry Scott, ASID
Design Lab
601 4th St., #125
San Francisco, CA 94107
(415) 974-1934

Clifford Selbert
Clifford Selbert Design
Collaborative
1067 Massachusetts Ave.
Cambridge, MA 02140
(617) 497-6605

Teresa Sevilla
105 Tunnel Rd.
Berkeley, CA 94705
(510) 548-2435

George S. Sexton III, IALD, IES
George Sexton Associates
3222 N St., N.W., 5th Floor
Washington, DC
(202) 337-1903

April Sheldon Design
477 Bryant St.
San Francisco, CA 94107
(415) 541-7773

Richard Sherer
Lakeside Development
1535 West Markey St.
Mequon, WI 53092
(414) 241-2300

Joanne Sheridan
Sturgeon Interiors
229 West Bender Rd.
Milwaukee, WI 53217
(414) 964-8288

George Sinclair
Sinclair & Associates, Inc.
15 North Ellsworth Ave.
Suite 100
San Mateo, CA 94401
(415) 348-6865

Tom Skradski, ASID, IALD
Lumenworks
1121 Ranleigh Way
Suite 100
Piedmont, CA 94610
(510) 835-7600

Linday Smallwood Interiors
111 F Town & Country Dr.
Danville, CA 94526
(510) 837-1312

David Allen Smith Architect
444 Pearl St., Suite B2
Monterey, CA 93940
(408) 373-7337

Greg Smith, ASID
JPS Design Group
501 Seaport Court
Suite 201
Redwood City, CA 94063
(415) 368-7711

Peter Smith, MRAIC
Lett Smith Architects
99 Crown Lane
Toronto, Ontario M5R 3P4
Canada
(416) 968-6990

Robin Snell
Michael Hopkins and Partners
27 Broadley Terrace
London, NW1 6LG England
01/1-724-1/51

Ruth Soforenko, ASID
Ruth Soforenko Associates
137 Forest Ave.
Palo Alto, CA 94301
(415) 326-5448

Michael Souter, ASID, IALD
Past President N. Calif. ASID
Luminae Souter Lighting Design
1740 Army St. 2nd Floor
San Francisco, CA 94124
(415) 285-2622

Charles Southall
Moore Andersson Architects
1801 North Lamar, #100
Austin, TX 78701
(512) 476-5780

Barbara Spandorf, AIA
Prentice & Chan, Ohlhausen
Architects
14 East 4th St.
New York, NY 10012
(212) 420-8600

Spectra F/X
1270 Avenida Acaso
Camarillo, CA 93012
(805) 388-5246

Gerry Stebnicki
Stebnicki Robertson and
Associates Ltd.
403, 1240 Kensington Rd., N.W.
Calgary, Alberta T2N 3P7 Canada
(403) 270-8833

Gordon Stein
Stein & Associates
49858 San Juan Ave.
Palm Desert, CA 92260
(760) 568-3696

Sylvia Stevens
Sylvia Stevens and Associates
2356 Jones St.
San Francisco, CA 94133
(415) 474-5815

Eric Stine Architect Inc.
1-1864 West 1st Ave.
Vancouver, BA V6J 1G5
Canada
(604) 732-4545

Victoria Stone Interiors
893 Noe St.
San Francisco, CA 94114
(415) 826-0904

David Story, IALS, IES
David Story Design
213 1st Ave., Suite 2B
Seattle, WA 98104
(206) 624-9189

Studios Architecture
99 Green St.
San Francisco, CA 94111
(415) 398-7575

Ron Sutton
Sutton-Suzuki
39 Forrest St.
Mill Valley, CA 94941
(415) 456-1656

Suzman Design Associates
233 Douglas St.
San Francisco, CA 94114
(415) 252-0111

Candida Tabet
Mantovani & Tabi Com. de
Moveis Ltda
Rua Medeiros de
Albuquerque, 23
Sao Paulo, Sao Paulo
05436-060 Brazil
011-55-11-211-0418

Takenaka Corporation
1-21-8 Ginza, Chuo-ku
Tokyo, 104 Japan
81-3-3542-7100

Seiji Tanaka
Yoshimura Architects &
Associates
28 Kamimiyanomae-cho
Shishigatani, Sakyo-ku
Kyoto, 606 Japan
011-81-075-771-6071

Loyd Ray Taylor
Loyd-Paxton Inc.
3636 Maple Ave.
Dallas, TX 75219
(214) 521-1521

Mark Thomas & Associates
444 Spear St.
San Francisco, CA 94105
(415) 495-2778

Charles K. Thompson, AIA,
IESNA, IALD
Archillume Lighting Design
3701 Executive Center Dr., #150
Austin, TX 78731
(512) 346-1386

Christopher Thompson
Tails Inc.
Full Spectrum Electrical and
Lighting Design
2605 Western Ave.
Seattle, WA 98121
(206) 443-9837

Jacqueline Thornton
Jacqueline & Associates
928 South Valley View
Las Vegas, NV 98107
(702) 877-9347

TL Yamagiwa Laboratory
4-15-7 Nishishinjuku, Shinjuku-ku
Tokyo Japan
03-5371-1640

TL Yamagiwa Laboratory
4-5-18 Higashinippori, Arakawa-ku
Tokyo, 116 Japan
03-3803-6859

Duncan Todd
414 Mason St., Suite 702
San Francisco, CA 94102
(415) 362-7670

Laura Tredinnick, IES
Schuler & Shook, Inc.
123 Third Street N., Suite 216
Minneapolis, MN 55401
(612) 339-5958

Robert Truax
Lighting Design and Consultation
360 Arguello Blvd.
San Francisco, CA 94118
(415) 668-0253

Stella Tuttle, ASID, CID
Tuttle & Associates
4155 El Camino Way, #2
Palo Alto, CA 94306
(415) 857-1171

Masahiko Uchiyama
Step Design
Product Planning & Design
5-18-19-503 Roppongi
Minato-ku
Tokyo, Japan
81-03-5562-0571

Stom Ushidate, DDA, JCD
Stom Ushidate + Interspace Time
Dai-ni Orient Building
5-13-11 Ueno Taito-ku
Tokyo, 110 Japan
03-3836-7293

Ushiospax
2-43-15 Tomigaya, Shibuya-ku
Tokyo, 151 Japan
03-5478-7411

Ravi Varma
RNM
4611 Teller Ave., #100
Newport Beach, CA 92660
(714) 262-0908

Joseph Vincent
Andrew Belschner Joseph Vincent
821 Sansome St.
San Francisco, CA 94111
(415) 982-1215

Lee von Hasseln
P.O. Box 213
Pebble Beach, CA 93953
(408) 625-6467

Jim Wallen
Acorn Kitchens and Baths
4640 Telegraph Ave.
Oakland, CA 94609
(510) 547-6581

Ward Young Architects
12010 Donner Pass Rd.
Truckee, CA 96161
(916) 587-3859

Cathy Wentz Interior Design
85 Stevenson Lane
Atherton, CA 94027
(415) 327-7009

William Whistler, AIA
Brennan Beer Gorman Monk /
Interiors
515 Madison Ave.
New York, NY 10022
(212) 888-7663

Randall Whitehead, IALD, ASID
Affiliate
Principal
Light Source Design Group
1246 18th St.
San Francisco, CA 94107
(415) 626-1210

Whitfield Partners
63/67 Carter Lane
London, EC4 5HE
United Kingdom

Dudley Williams
Wheatman & Associates
1933 Union St.
San Francisco, CA 94123
(415) 346-8300

Stephen Wilmot
4114 El Bosque Dr.
Pebble Beach, CA 93953
(408) 625-5399

Trisha Wilson
Trisha Wilson
3811 Turtle Creek Blvd.,
15th Floor
Dallas, TX 75219
(214) 521-6753

Wimberly Allison Tong & Goo
2260 University Dr.
Newport Beach, CA 92660
(714) 574-8500

Deborah Witte, Designer
Luminae Souter Lighting Design
1740 Army St., 2nd Floor
San Francisco, CA 94124
(415) 285-2622

Wil Wong
Wil Wong Associates
2710 Webster St.
San Francisco, CA 94123
(415) 346-7700

Evans Woollen
Woollen, Molzan and Partner, Inc.
47 South Pensylvania St.
10th Floor
Indianapolis, IN 46204
(317) 632 7484

Jack J. Worstell, AIA
Hornberger + Worstell
170 Maiden Lane, Suite 170
San Francisco, CA 94108
(415) 391-1080

Christian Wright
Robert Hering & Associates
151 Vermont St., #7
San Francisco, CA 94103
(415) 863-4144

Greg Yale
Landscape Illumination
27 Henry Rd.
South Hampton, NY 11968
(516) 287-2132

Michi Yamaguchi, AIA
RTKL Associates Inc.
Commerce Place One South St.
Baltimore, MD 21202
(410) 528-8600

Jeffrey Werner, ASID
Werner Design Associates
35 Yorkshire Lane
Redwood City, CA 94062
(415) 367-9033

Paul Zaferiou
Lam Partners Inc.
84 Sherman St.
Cambridge, MA 02140
(617) 354-4502

Alfredo Zaparolli
Techlinea Design Associates
2325 3rd St, Suite 430
San Francisco, CA 94107
(415) 863-7773

Directory of Photographers

Russell Abraham Photography
60 Federal St., Suite 303
San Francisco, CA 94107
(415) 896-6400

Anthony P. Albarello
80 Blackwells Mills Rd.
Somerset, NJ 08873
(908) 873-0319

Dennis Anderson Photography
48 Lucky Dr.
Greenbrae, CA 94904
(415) 927-3530

Yoshihisa Araki
Atelier Fukumoto Co.
301 Crest Shinsaibashi 4-12-9
Minamisenba, Chuo-Ku
Osaka, Osaka 542 Japan
011-81-06-245-4680

Jaime Ardiles-Arce
663 Fifth Ave.
New York, NY 10022
(212) 371-4749

Thomas Arledge
Arledge Studios
11616 Regency Dr.
Potomac, MD 20854
(301) 983-5226

Chris Arthur
Transworld Eye
64 Gloucester Rd.
Kingston-Upon-Thames, KTI 3RB
United Kingdom
44-0181-546-4066

Fashid Assassi
Assassi Productions
P.O. Box 3651
Santa Barbara, CA 93130
(805) 682-2158

Yoshiteru Baba
Nacasa & Partners Inc.
3-5-5 Minami Azabu, Minato-Ku
Tokyo, 106 Japan
03-3444-2922

Paul Bardagjy Photography
4111 Marathon Blvd.
Austin, TX 78756
(512) 452-9636

Richard Barnes
John Barnes Photography
1403 Shotwell
San Francisco, CA 94110
(415) 550-1023

Patrick Barta Photography
80 S. Washington St., Suite 204
Seattle, WA 98104
(206) 343-7644

Waldo Bascom Photography
26 Medway Rd.
San Rafael, CA 94901
(415) 456-1262

Batista Moon Studio
10 Cillo Vista Dr.
Monterey, CA 93940
(408) 373-1947

Robert Bengtson Photography
8A Ridge Ave.
Mill Valley, CA 94941
(415) 380-8486

John Benson Photography
130 Ninth St.
San Francisco, CA 94103
(415) 621-5247

Rosalie Blakey Wardell
Photography
3435 Army St., #322
San Francisco, CA 94110
(415) 641-6271

Jeff Blanton Photography
5515 South Orange Ave.
Orlando, FL 32809
(407) 851-7279

Michael Bruk
Photo/Graphics
731 Florida St.
Studio 201
San Francisco, CA 94110
(415) 824-8600

Robert Burley
Design Archive
276 Carlaw Ave., Suite 219
Toronto, Ontario M4M 2L1
Canada
(416) 466-0211

John Canham
Quadra Focus
588 Waite Ave.
Sunnyvale, CA 94086
(408) 739-1465

John Casado Photography
477 Bryant St.
San Francisco, CA 94107
(415) 284-0164

Dave Chawla Associates
P.O. Box 26931
Las Vegas, NY 89126
(702) 253-6306

Langdon Clay
2221 Peachtree Rd. N.E.
Suite D-195
Atlanta, GA 30309
(404) 916-7265

David Clifton
David Clifton Photography
2637 W. Winnemec St.
Chicago, IL 60625
(312) 334-4346

Beatriz Coll
Coll Photography
2415 3rd St.
San Francisco, CA 94107
(415) 863-0699

Robert Ames Cook Photography
809 Hickory Highland Dr.
Antioch, TN 37013
(615) 591-3270

Charles Cormany
845 5th Ave.
San Rafael, CA 94901
(415) 455-8784

Mark Darley
311 Seymour Lane
Mill Valley, CA 94941
(415) 381-5452

Gil Edelstein Photography
4120 Matisse Ave.
Woodland Hills, CA 91364
(818) 716-8909

Engelhardt and Sellin
Postfach 120, 8000 Muchen 65
Germany
49-89-811-3903

Martin Fine
10072 Larwin Ave. #1
Chatsworth, CA 91322
(818) 341-7113

Dan Forer
Forer, Inc.
1970 N.E. 149th St.
North Miami, FL 33181
(305) 949-3131

Stephen Fridge
Fridge Photography
325 9th St.
San Francisco, CA 94103
(415) 552-6754

Atelier Fukumoto
4-12-9-301 Minami Senba,
Chuo-ku
Osaka Japan
81-06-245-4680

Masaaki Fukumoto
Atelier Fukumoto Company
301 Crest Shinsaibachi
12-9, 4-Chome Minanisemha,
Chuo-ku
Osaka, 542 Japan
06-245-4680

Andrew Garn
Andrew Garn Photography
85 E. 10th St.
New York, NY 10003
(212) 353-8434

Dennis Gilbert
11 Furmage St.
London, SW18 4DF
United Kingdom
0181-870-9051

Jeff Goldberg
Esto Photographics
222 Valley Place
Mamaroneck, NY 10543
(914) 698-4060

Jay Graham Photography
P.O. Box 1607
San Anselmo, CA 94960
(415) 459-3839

J.B. Grant
508 67th St.
West New York, NJ 07093
(201) 854-1785

Anton Grassl
5 Sycamore St.
Cambridge, MA 02140
(617) 876-1321

Mark Gubin
K & S Photographies
250 Northwater St.
Milwaukee, WI 53202
(414) 271-6004

Steven Hall
Hedrich-Blessing
11 West Illinois St.
Chicago, IL 60610
(312) 321-1151

Philip Harvey Photography
911 Minna St.
San Francisco, CA 94103
(415) 861-2188

Mark F. Heffron
Heffoto
P.O. Box 700
Milwaukee, WI 53202
(414) 962-0719

George Heinrich
1516 S. 7th St.
Minneapolis, MN 55454
(612) 338-2092

Christopher Irion
183 Shipley St.
San Francisco, CA 94107
(415) 896-0752

Ben Janken Photography
48 Agnon Ave.
San Francisco, CA 94112
(415) 206-1645

Douglas Johnson Photography
P.O. Box 984
Danville, CA 94526
(510) 837-4482

Elliot Kaufman
Elliot Kaufman
255 W. 90th St.
New York, NY 10024
(212) 496-0860

Steve Keating
Steve Keating Photography
3411-A 33rd Ave. W.
Seattle, WA 98199
(206) 282-6506

Cecile Keefe Photography
P.O. box 193367
San Francisco, CA 94119
(415) 647-3330

Donna Kempner
P.O. Box 421190
San Francisco, CA 94142
(415) 771-1326

Muffy Kibbey Photography
3036 Hillegass Ave.
Berkeley, CA 94705
(510) 549-1115

Klein & Wilson
7015 San Mateo Blvd.
Dallas, TX 75223
(214) 328-8627

Balthazar Korab
P.O. Box 895
Troy, MI 48099-0985
(313) 641-8881

Christian Korab
Balthazar Korab, Ltd.
2757 Emerson Ave. S.
Minneapolis, MN 55408

Michael L. Krasnobrod
Fotek
3499 Sacramento St.
San Francisco, CA 94118

Chris A. Little
P.O. Box 4067221
Atlanta, GA 30346
(404) 641-9688

David Livingston Photography
1036 Erica Rd.
Mill Valley, CA 94941
(415) 383-0898

Tim Long
Long Photography
Chicago, IL
(312) 718-5118

Marco Lorenzetti
C/o Hedrich Blessing
11 West Illinois St.
Chicago, IL 60610
(312) 321-1151

Michael Lowry
2471 John Young Parkway
Orlando, FL 32804
(407) 291-1464

John Martin Photography
68 Ashton Ave.
San Francisco, CA 94112
(415) 337-7408

Chas McGrath Photography
3735 Kansas Dr.
Santa Rosa, CA 95405
(707) 545-5853

Nick Merrick
C/o Hedrich Blessing
11 West Illinois St.
Chicago, IL 60610
(312) 321-1151

Fred Milkie
Milkie Studio
127 Boylston Ave. E.
Seattle, WA 98102
(206) 324-3000

Jon Miller
C/o Hedrich Blessing
11 West Illinois St.
Chicago, IL 60610
(312) 321-1151

Helmut Mitter
Weintraubengasse 14 / 10 A-1020
Vienna Austria
01143-1-21-404-53

Ira Montgomery Photography
2406 Converse
Dallas, TX 75207
(214) 638-7288

Nacasa & Partners Inc.
3-5-5 Minami Azabu, Minato-ku
Tokyo, 106 Japan
03-3444-2922

Mary E. Nichols
722 N. Arden Blvd.
Los Angeles, CA 90004
(213) 871-0770

Toshitaka Niwa
Universe
Rm 302, Shiguma Royal
Hights, 3-5-7, Yoyogi
Shibuya-ku, Tokyo, Japan 151
81-3-3373-4709

Andres Otero
Blick Producoes
Av. Higienopolis, 578/87
Sao Paulo, Sao Paulo
01238-000 Brazil
011-55-11-824-0779

Gary Otte
Foto: Otte Photographer
21-1551 Johnston St.
Granville Island
Vancouver, BC U6H 3R9
Canada
(604) 681-8421

Eric Oxendorf Studio
1442 North Franklin Place
Milwaukee, WI 53202
(414) 273-0654

Peter Paige
Peter Paige Photography
269 Parkside Rd.
Harrington Park, NJ 07640
(201) 767-3150

Philip Pavliger Photography
9 Decatur
San Francisco, CA 94103
(415) 896-6486

Robert Pisano
Robert Pisano Photography
7527 15th Ave. N.E.
Seattle, WA 98115
(206) 525-3500

Tuca Reines Estudio
Fotografico Ltda
Rua Emanoel Kant, 58
Sao Paulo, Sao Paulo
04536-050 Brazil
011-55-11-3061-9127

Kenneth Rice Photography
456 61st St.
Oakland, CA 94103
(510) 652-1752

Sharon Risedorph Photography
761 Clementina St.
San Francisco, CA 94103
(415) 431-5851

Brian Rose
Prentice & Chan, Ohlhausen
14 E. 4th St.
New York, NY 10012
(212) 420-8600

Cesar Rubio
2565 Third St.
San Francisco, CA 94107
(415) 550-6369

Douglas Salin Photography
647 Joost Ave.
San Francisco, CA 94127
(415) 584-3322

Durston Saylor
14 E. 4th St., Suite 1118
New York, NY 10012
(212) 228-2468

Yoshio Shiratori
ZOOM
505 5-3 Minamimotomachi,
Shinjuku-ku
Tokyo, 160 Japan
03-3353-0442

Ron Starr Photography
4104 24th St., #358
San Francisco, CA 94114
(415) 541-7732

David Story
213 1st Ave. S, Suite 2B
Seattle, WA 98104
(206) 624-9189

John Sutton Photography
8 Main St.
Point San Quentin, CA 94964
(415) 258-8100

Robert Swanson
Swanson Images
532 Lisbon St.
San Francisco, CA 94112
(415) 585-6567

Toshiya Toyoda
Toyoda Photo Studio
1-3611 Sakuraoka, Shime-cho
Kasuyagun, Fukuoka 811-ZZ
Japan 811-22
011-092-935-7987

Masanori Umeda
U-Meta Design, Inc.
1-8-3 Nishiazabu, Minato-ku
Tokyo, 108 Japan
03-3401-0328

John Vaughan Photography
5242 Reedley Way
Hayward, CA 94546
(510) 481-9814

Hector Jorge Verdecchia
Monroe 1737
Buenos Aires, 1737
Argentina
541-784-9574

Peter Vitale
208 E. 60th St.
New York, NY 10022
(212) 888-6409

Paul Warchol
Paul Warchol
133 Mulberry St., Apt. #6 S.
New York, NY 10013
(212) 431-3461

Matthew Weinreb
16 Millfield Lane
London, N6 6JD
United Kingdom
0181-340-6690

Alan Weintraub Photography
1832 A Mason St.
San Francisco, CA 94114
(415) 553-8191

David Whitcomb
RTKL Associates Inc.
Commerce Place,
One South St.
Baltimore, MD 21202
(410) 528-8600

Steve Whittaker
Whittaker Photography
1155 Chess Dr., Bldg. C
Suite 125
Foster City, CA 94404
(415) 574-5424

Tom Wyatt
Sunset Publishing Co.
80 Willow Rd.
Menlo Park, CA 94025
(415) 321-3600

Yamagiwa Corporation
4-5-18 Higashi Nippori Arakawaku
Tokyo Japan
3-3803-6877

Eric Zepeda
4X5
1451 Stevenson St., Studio A
San Francisco, CA 94103
(415) 558-9691

Scott Zimmerman
Architectural Photography
P.O. Box 289
Heber City, UT 84032
(801) 279-2757